THE LAST LOVE OF EDITH PIAF

CHRISTIE LAUME

THE LAST LOVE OF EDITH PIAF

translated from French
by Jean Gill

l'Archipel

Our catalogue is available at
www.editionsarchipel.com

Éditions de l'Archipel
34, rue des Bourdonnais
75001 Paris

EAN 9782809816334

To my children and my grandchildren

Mais toi, t'es le dernier,
Mais toi, t'es le premier !

(« À quoi ça sert l'amour ? »)

It's you, who are the last one,
And it's you, who are the first!

(« What's the point of love »)

Prologue

I was twenty when, in the back room of the family hairdressing salon, my brother Théo asked me one day, 'See that telephone, Christie? At 6 p.m. in a few minutes, it's going to ring. And do you know who'll be at the other end?'

I waited for the punch-line because Théo was looking at me so intently.

'Edith Piaf.'

He loved playing tricks on me. It was probably one of his favourite activities. He took advantage of my unconditional love for him to lead me on many a wild goose chase. This time, though, the joke was a bit too big to swallow and I had difficulty believing him.

Edith Piaf...

Even at that time, long before the film starring Marion Cotillard, everyone knew of the entertainer from Belleville, born in poverty, who became a living legend in a manner of speaking the very incarnation of French *chanson*. The Little Sparrow! Not one day went by without *Milord, Non, je ne regrette rien* or *L'homme à la moto* being played on the radio. Even her private life was followed by the French public, who seemed to believe they had an intimate relationship with her. The newspapers had covered in detail her love affair with the entertainer Yves Montand, then with the boxer Marcel Cerdan, who was lost in a plane crash. Marlene Dietrich had been a witness at her wedding to singer Jacques Pills, in 1952, in New York. Her entourage included names famous from the music-hall: Charles Aznavour, Georges Moustaki, Bruno Coquatrix. She had given a memorable series of concerts at Olympia. Her health was said to be fragile and her vulnerable side – an unforgettable voice soaring from a body in pain, ill-treated – elicited even more sympathy from the public.

I repeated, 'Edith Piaf…?'

Théo, who saw that I was sceptical and read my thoughts like an open book, repeated his prediction. 'Wait and see. At six o'clock, the telephone will ring. You're going to answer, pick up the phone, hold it against your ear but without saying anything! You'll pass it to me straightaway.'

He seemed so serious! Perhaps it was true after all… but if that was so, I couldn't imagine any reason why the great Edith Piaf, the renowned entertainer, would call my brother Théo at home.

I looked at the clock fixed on the wall. Théo said nothing more. He seemed tense.

Suddenly, the sound of the telephone rose up from the filing tray where our father organised his paperwork. With a nervous gesture, my brother motioned to me to pick it up. I took the phone off the hook, held it to my ear. I heard a deep voice.

'Hello…'

Quickly, I passed the phone to my brother, who tore it out of my hand and indicated that I should leave.

I went into the garden. I was on pins with curiosity, so much so that my heart was racing. I thought I had indeed recognized the voice of the Little Sparrow down the line.

I waited. Inside, the conversation dragged on forever. I fretted. I wanted to know every last word in this story! My brother finally came out to join me. He was radiant.

'Well, what did I tell you?'

I had a million questions to ask but he didn't give me time to figure out how to express the first one.

'I have to hurry. I've been invited over to her place. With all her friends.'

'You're invited to Edith Piaf's?'

This time, I didn't doubt him. But he wasn't listening. He'd already turned his back on me, leaving me rooted to the spot, and dashed back into the house. He was in a rush to get changed and charge off to his rendez-vous, completely innocent when it came to how this would change his life – and that of family.

1

I was born in Paris in occupied France on February 4th, 1942, in the middle of the Second World War.

My parents were Greek. My father's family, the Lamboukas, came from the Isle of Marmara in Turkey. My grandmother, who was called Yaya, could never talk about Marmara without shedding a nostalgic tear. I can still hear her describing to me the way a Turkish marriage is carried out the men restricted to the ground floor, the women upstairs, where they were allowed to take off their veils. Yaya loved Turkey and Greece equally, and the war which pitted her two countries against each other drove her to despair. Even more so because the conflict had killed her husband when she was only thirty. They had four children, including my father, Stavros, who was nine at the time.

My grandfather, a sick man, had been discharged from the Turkish army didn't given time to get treatment; soldiers came to sign him up once more, taking him away and beating him up in front of his wife and children. Grandfather had to come home again shortly afterwards, suffering from dysentery.

Yaya begged the doctor to save him. His services always came with the demand for ever more remuneration in gold coins. Finally, he could do no more. And Yaya lost her husband. She was also to lose one of her four children.

Yaya, born into a shipping family, had a little money: the famous gold coins she kept sewn into her long, black skirt. She was generous not only with her own children, but also with other people's when they were hungry leaving hunks of bread she has baked on the windowsill for them. When there was no bread left beside the window, she used to hear the children calling to her from outside. 'Mia! Give us some bread! Mia! We're starving!' Their stomachs were bloated not because they'd eaten too much, but because there was no food for them.

Yaya's little stash soon melted almost completely away. This prompted my father to think of leaving. Having prepared his small suitcase in secret, he left the house in the middle of the night, leaving a letter to his mother on the dresser. He told her that he was leaving for Paris in the hope of working for his uncle who ran a restaurant there. He promised to send her money.

That same day, my father approached a freighter captain he'd met before. Knowing that the boat made a stop at Marseilles, Papa asked for permission to embark. The captain was reluctant to agree.

'You are very young, Stavros. I don't want comebacks.'

Papa slipped a little money into his hand and the captain let himself be swayed my father could climb aboard as a stowaway. He spent the whole voyage hidden under a tarpaulin. After a few days, he disembarked at Marseilles heading straight for Saint-Charles Station to catch the train for Paris. At Paris Gare de Lyon, he jumped into a taxi showing the driver the name of his uncle's restaurant, wich was well-known. Once there, Papa introduced himself.

'I'm Stavros Lamboukas.'

My uncle put him to work right there and then.

However, Stavros didn't get the chance to send his mother money, because the Turks in Marmara had decided they wanted the Greeks out. Two million of them were duly chased out of Turkey, the country where many were born. Aware of the threat was growing closer and closer, Yaya realised that it was time to leave. She counted the few coins still sewn into the hem of her skirt, organised her affairs and said goodbye to the house which held so many memories, taking her children with her. As a result, Papa soon saw his mother joining him in Paris, along with his sister and brother.

Everyone moved into the same apartment on rue Cadet.

By this time Papa was tired of his uncle's restaurant, where the work was thankless and the pay inadequate. His dream was to become a lawyer, but the training was too expensive and he had no means of paying. He had taken a course in hairdressing and sometimes said he thought there might be a future for him in this line of work, especially because he was always well turned-out, as well as being bold and intelligent. One day, when he was leafing through the newspapers, he came across a small ad '*Hairdressing school seeks teacher*'. Papa didn't have a diploma. In addition, there was an entry exam. But sometimes fortune does favour the brave. The exam required him to style the hair of a female model. When he started work, everyone in the salon crowded around to admire his way of working. This is how he became a teacher of hairdressing for women!

It became clear that he'd made a good choice, as he soon started to make a decent living. Before long, he was able to buy a new place to live on rue de Provence. The apartment was huge, with two rooms converted into hairdressing salons. His clientèle was made up of women who knew him by word of mouth, because his name was passed round at the big department stores, Printemps and Galeries Lafayette, which were just around the corner. Papa's salon was incredibly successful, but this did not please the Director of the hairdressing school, who proceeded to sue him. Papa hired an advocate to defend him, but the man was so incompetent that my father thanked him and decided to represent himself. By pleading his own cause, he won the lawsuit. Along with its other benefits, this victory allowed him to realise what had long been his most cherished dream to exercise the profession of advocate – albeit temporarily.

In 1934, my Aunt Anna, my father's sister, went to Kavala in the north of Greece on her honeymoon. During this visit, she struck up a friendship with Marika, a young girl of sixteen, to whom she inevitably spoke at length about her brother, Stavros, at this stage a bachelor in Paris. Marika gave Anna a photo of herself, which was duly shown to Stavros when his sister returned home. Stavros thought the young girl's features were attractive and so more photos were exchanged, as well as letters. Finally, Stavros asked for Marika's hand in marriage. The young woman carefully considered the portrait sent to her. Her suitor was thirteen years older than her but she concluded that she was dealing with a man of integrity, who had made sure the photo showed him bare-headed, so he wouldn't be suspected of hiding grey hairs or a receding hairline. After much thought, Marika headed for Paris to marry Stavros. She would never regret the decision. It's true that she was never *madly* in love with Papa, but she did love him and gave him all of her affection. Her judgement had not let her down: Stavros was trustworthy hard-working, and tidy enough to reassure a woman. Their marriage took place in 1935. The next year, their first child saw the light of day: Théophanis, known as Théo.

Stavros, Marika, baby Théo and Grandma Yaya were still living in the same apartment on rue de Provence. My father could never say no to a client and his working days were full to bursting. Maman worked at the salon too. In summer, everyone needed to get away from Paris on Sundays. Their favourite places were in Seine-et-Oise, Herblay and La Frette-sur-Seine. When they realised their savings would enable them to buy a second home, their choice was La Frette, a hilltop village twenty minutes from the capital. It was especially charming as a place with its little Town Hall, a church, a café where everyone met up with friends over a glass of wine, a patisserie selling enough pastries to keep the children happy, and a tree-lined walk going down to the Seine. It was the ideal backdrop for relaxed family weekends. It was also a meeting-place for artists; many painters set up their easels in the village, in imitation of Monet, who had been inspired by the landscapes around and about.

Yet the spectre of war, which had brought Yaya so much suffering, loomed once more. My brother Théo was only three years old when the Germans occupied France, and my grandmother left Paris to look after him in La Frette. My parents joined them there every weekend.

One day, Papa received a phone call from Yaya when he was at work. She had rushed to the café with Théo and asked to use the phone there.

'You have to come at once, Stavros! The Germans want to move into the house!'

Stavros and Marika dashed to Saint-Lazare station and jumped on the first train for La Frette. When they arrived, there were indeed soldiers in the act of moving into the house. Judging it better to negotiate, Papa made a suggestion to the officer in charge.

'Why don't you take the first floor? We'll keep the ground floor.'

Papa made himself cough all night. The noise woke Théo, who started crying. In the morning, the Germans came out of their rooms and headed downstairs, where Stavros was waiting.

'Did you sleep well, gentlemen?'
'Nein.'
The same charade was repeated every night. After a few days, the officer said to my father, 'Your house is too noisy.'
The decision was made; they moved out.
At the beginning of 1942, Maman was expecting a baby. In February, she was at work in the hairdressing salon on rue de Provence at the end of the day when she felt the first contractions. As there was a curfew in place at this time in Paris, no-one had the right to leave the house and there were certainly there were no taxis on the roads. It was vital to get to the hospital but how could they manage this? Maman was in pain Papa was thinking aloud. A woman from the apartment block who'd come for a hairdo was there and had a sudden idea.
'Call the Kommandantur!'
My father looked at her, puzzled.
'What else? Call the Kommandantur, Monsieur Lamboukas. Tell them that your wife is about to give birth. This is a situation for the big guns, no?'
The argument convinced Papa, who took the phone off the hook and did as his client suggested.
Shortly afterwards, two German officers arrived at the apartment. Their car was parked outside, on rue de Provence in front of the building and they invited Papa and Maman to follow them. Maman felt terrible, doubled up with pain, but she suffered in silence. Papa held her hand the whole journey. The car headed first towards the 15th arrondissement and Necker Hospital, where my brother was born. The

officers went personally to get instructions but came back saying they were sorry; the maternity unit was over its capacity so they would have to go to Hotel-Dieu in the 4th arrondissement. With Maman suffering more and more, the car went back across the Seine.

This was in a different time and during a war; as soon as she'd given birth, Maman left with her baby to recover at home. To get back from the hospital and return to rue de Provence, did Papa call the Kommandantur a second time? No: I began my life with a tour of Paris in a horse-drawn carriage. Apparently, the streets were white with snow. I'd been covered with a blanket and, to keep me warm, Maman hugged me tightly to her.

During the liberation of Paris, Maman took me to the Orthodox Church on rue Georges-Bizet, where she had married my father Théo had been baptised there. I was three years old and it was my turn now. It was a hot day and the air was heavy with incense. At that time, the priest said mass in ancient Greek. My parents lifted me up to kiss the icons. Then Maman and my godmother took off my clothes. Was I going to be examined by a doctor? No, it was the priest who took me in his arms and immersed me three times in the copper font before he anointed me with oils. All my mother had to do then was to dress me again in my pretty white dress. While the family was leaving the church, we came across some Americans, who asked Papa for permission to take photos of our lively, happy group. Two officers asked Papa to photograph them while one of them held me in his arms. My parents always said they felt honoured by the incident: their daughter photographed in the arms of the soldiers who'd come to liberate Europe.

The baptism celebration included many residents of La Frette. My parents liked well-dressed tables and the guests were brought together for lunch in the living-room, complete a white tablecloth, crystal glasses, silver place settings and Limoges china. The celebration of the baptism was enhanced by joy at being at peace once more. It goes without saying that Papa was generous with wine and champagne!

The meal was supposed to be followed by some entertainment, organised by Théo, who, at nine years old, was inclined to put on shows. We used the entrance to the house for the performance and the French windows which separated it from the lounge turned it into the perfect stage. Accompanied by my cousin, I sang the song made famous by Georges Ulmer that Théo had made us rehearse endlessly:

> *Quand allons-nous marier, nous marier, nous marier,*
> *Quand allons-nous marier, nous marier, mon Cowboy adoré ?*
>
> *(When will the wedding be, the wedding be, the wedding be,*
> *When will the wedding be, my beloved Cowboy?)*

Warm applause. However, at the end of the performance, conversations about the war started up again; the conflict might well have been over, but it was still in everyone's head.

A bit later, a client of my father's gave him the use of a house she owned in Normandy. I still remember that journey as a happy occasion uniting two families: my parents, my grandmother, my brother Théo, my uncle, my aunt, my cousins. I can still see Saint-Lazare station as if it were yesterday: the vendors rooth sandwiches and drinks; the train with compartments and net racks to store your luggage; the slow starting motion of the steam locomotive as the echoes of the whistle faded. It was all so different from the suburban trains that we were accustomed to catching! Suddenly, I felt like I was really heading off on a big adventure. Our destination was Caen. The town had been decimated by bombardments, like so much of Normandy. A bus carried us to Ouistreham and Riva Bella, where the famous house was waiting for us. To our surprise, it had been badly damaged by the war the windows were smashed and it had been ransacked. In fact, only the walls and roof were still standing. In the surrounding region, many families were living in a similar way in partly destroyed houses. Papa inspected the place, then turned to us children and asked, 'What do you want to do? Go back to Paris?'

'No! No way!'

'Then it looks like we're camping.'

And we rushed off straight away to the sea-side, which I saw that day for the first time. We ran on the fine sands, played in the wartime blockhouse, bathed in the sea and came out shivering, to wrap ourselves in the towels our parents held out to us. From then on, we all took the train for Normandy every summer. We were accompanied by Yaya, who, from old habit, kept her money tucked into her bra, secured with a safety-pin. However, my parents were always careful after that summer to rent a house in good condition. They even ended up buying one!

We also spent part of the summer at La Frette, where we made the most of a garden planted with lime trees. Papa, who always rose early, watered the flowers and the vegetable patch. When we woke up, Théo and I went outside in our pyjamas to run on the grass and nibble on a tomato. We would then go back into the house, where the smell of coffee – Greek coffee, obviously – wafted past. Maman would make toast; slices of day-old bread browned under the grill. Yaya made jam with plums from the garden. But sometimes before breakfast, Théo and I would be 'entitled' to a large spoonful of cod-liver oil! We had to pinch our noses to cope with the stench!

At La Frette, the garden played a very important rôle in our lives. Mealtimes, for the most part, took place outside. On summer evenings, after dinner, Papa would take up his guitar, for which he only knew one chord, and he would accompany Maman's singing. She had a lovely voice. All the while, Yaya would nod her head with a nostalgic expression on her face. Their repertoire was Greek and French. No doubt these moments of harmony played their rôle in Théo's future vocation, and mine too.

After a moment, I would say, 'Where is Théo?'

'Hiding in a lime tree,' my mother would reply. 'But hush, don't say anything. He doesn't think we can see him.'

Théo was a boisterous child. He made a swing by attaching a taut wire in the garden between two columns of bricks, which didn't stand up to the task for very long. He liked climbing trees and listening to music in secret, always lost in his own dreams.

Our parents weren't regular churchgoers: only Yaya went to mass every Sunday. But we were believers in our family. There were icons in the house and we were lifted up off the ground when instructed to kiss them. There were also biblical phrases which seemed to drop of their own accord from my father's mouth. Papa quoted scripture naturally, and sayings from St Paul and the Gospels were slipped into his everyday conversation. I can still see him making the sign of the cross before eating.

When Easter came, THE holiday of holidays, Maman went to the Greek church on Good Friday. Then, with my grandmother, she created red eggs and the sugared bread called *koulourias*. Before the cake was cut, a cross was carved into the top with a knife. The first slice was for the Father, the second for the Son, the third for the Holy Ghost, the fourth for any elderly people present, and so it continued. These were the religious elements that formed part of our lives in a household where both our father and mother had been to orthodox schools. At that time, I had no worries about God or churches. Round about my sixteenth birthday, thought I was taken with the idea of entering holy orders, but my brother made fun of this whim and I immediately stopped thinking about it. Nevertheless, a grounding in

Christianity had been passed on to me, which would then flourish years later.

In the village, where Papa was known as 'Monsieur Max', we used to go to the baker's, which smelled of baguettes fresh from the oven; the market; the news-stand; and the grocer's, where Théo and I used to love buying balls of chewing-gum and the famous Pierrot Gourmand caramel lollipops. I also remember a mysterious character, wearing a hat and dressed in a black velvet cape who frightened me a little at first. This man lived opposite the school in a huge mansion which overlooked the Seine. Our paths would often cross when I was going to school and he would say, 'You shouldn't eat sweets or you'll spoil your teeth.'

I had the impression he'd discovered my secret from when I was little, it was true that I needed to suck a sweet before going to sleep. 'How did you know I like sweets?' I asked him.

'All children like them.'

As I later found out, this man was a famous writer called Jacques Chardonne. The author of *L'Epithalame*, he had figured at the forefront of literary circles before the war and had continued to live in La Frette.

The market square was often the site for a funfair or circus. These were tiny affairs with two horses, three dogs, an acrobat, a clown. The fairground workers always included a stop in our village, knowing that they could count on my mother's generosity if they needed something.

Each year, La Frette also organised a Lilac Fête. Volunteers decorated cars and horse-drawn floats.

Théo and I were always first in line for these activities, even for the procession of Chinese lanterns, when the whole village paraded behind the local brass band. On the evening of the 14th July, the date of the National Fête, everyone used to go to the ball, and I can still remember a scene that was often repeated: our parents dancing together while Théo and I watched them, feeling emotional.

Maman had left her parents at the age of seventeen to live in France. They had died during the war, without her ever having had the chance to see them again. She felt homesick for her family, which is why one day she wanted to visit her sister, who was married to a Greek and had two children. They lived in Egypt, in Alexandria. Maman was away for a whole month. During this time, Théo, myself and my little sister, who was still a baby, were living at La Frette with Yaya. Each evening, after work, Papa caught the train to join us.

One evening, he took us, Théo and me, to the circus in the square. When I got back home, I was running a high temperature. Papa called the doctor out and I was duly examined. It then seemed to me that there were hushed conversations all around the house, but I was too ill to listen in to what was being said and I fell asleep without knowing what was wrong with me. When I awoke, I realised that I'd been moved onto the ground floor, into the morning room. I could see the lime trees and the flowers in the garden through the window. I was not allowed to go outside. The doctor arrived, accompanied by a nurse, who carried needles and a medicine box made of iron.

Both of them wore white coats, like in hospital. They gave me three really painful injections. Then Yaya told me that my father was going to speak to me. He came into the morning room, dressed in a white shirt, him too. He was even wearing gloves! He sat on the edge of my bed and asked me how I felt.

'The shots hurt!'

'You're ill, darling. You have diphtheria. It's a very contagious disease.'

During this episode, the hardest thing to bear was that Théo was not allowed into my room. We couldn't confide in each other or laugh together. We could only communicate through the window when he was in the garden. It was frustrating because we were so close. I was seven and he was thirteen. Aproaching adolescence, he was already very good-looking. Of course, I hero-worshipped him. He knew so many things of which I was ignorant as yet. He read a great deal. He was planning to study literature but was worried as to whether our father would approve. I loved his creative side, which perfectly expressed our family's yearning for the past. And I also loved the way Théo made me feel protected.

We had to get used to this new situation though. When he came home from school, Théo would put his schoolbag down in his room and then come back down into the garden to exchange a few words with me through the closed window. His dark hair made a magnificent contrast with the flowers and greenery of the background. He would play the clown just for me and mime silliness which brought tears to my eyes from laughing. I was entertained, having a good time watching my favourite actor. Finally, I wasn't bored stiff! At last, there was a distraction from this antiseptic universe of pain, peopled with nurses and injections. After a while, I would ask him through the window, 'What are you going to have to eat tonight?'

He would invariably give me the same reply, carefully articulating to make sure I'd understood, 'Vegetable soup, like you!'

Vegetable soup; I wasn't allowed anything else and he wanted to spare my feelings.

I was the only person in the village to be contaminated, hence the quarantine and precautionary measures. Thanks to the little mirror beside my bed, I could analyse the evolution of the white spots at the base of my throat.

After a month, Yaya took the phone off the hook, called Papa and said, 'It's finished, Stavros.'

Thinking that Yaya was announcing my death, Papa felt his blood freeze. But what she meant to say was that I was cured! The time had come to disinfect the room and throw away everything that carried a risk of contamination. Workers came to the house with buckets of disinfectant and rolls of adhesive paper to make the windows draught-proof. The whole room was covered in white powder. Yes, it really was over. I was no longer ill. I knew the joy of talking to Théo again, who, when he came back from high school, said to me, 'Look, I've got a surprise for you.'

He took me into the garden, beyond the lime trees. However, after a few steps, my strength let me down; I was still feeble, convalescing. Théo carried me in his arms as far as a shed that he had built for me with lime branches three walls, a roof, one side open. Inside he had put a table and two chairs. The table was laid. Everything was ready to make a meal: tomatoes, cucumbers, strawberries. Théo made me sit down, saying happily, 'Goodbye vegetable soup!'

He'd even brought a pack of cards to play a game after the meal.

A few days later, Maman came back from Egypt. The telegrams Papa had sent had never reached her. She had no idea that I'd had diphtheria. Horrified by the news, she swore she would never again travel without her children.

2

Théo had to enrol in a business school in Paris even though his leanings were towards literature and music. The fears he'd expressed when young proved to be well-founded our parents wanted him to take over the hairdressing salon. Such was the future they envisaged for him.

So he studied business, reluctantly, but that didn't stop him practising his talent for seduction. This meant he was in the habit of going to the cinema with a young salon employee, who was very pretty. Unfortunately, our uncle saw the turtle-doves on the bus and denounced them to my father, who flew into a rage with Théo.

'You should be concentrating on your studies! There's time enough to go out with girls when you come of age!'

Bear in mind that at this time 'coming of age' was at twenty-one! Théo protested, 'But Papa, you were only sixteen when you set off for Paris! And you did whatever you liked. You were free! Why should I wait till I'm twenty-one?'

'You think I did whatever I liked? I was forced to leave Turkey! And after that I had to work to support my family!'

Papa could see that Théo wanted to behave as a man, but, as a good father, had to do all he could to protect his son. They also came from two very different generations. Papa had grown up in Turkey, worlds away from the casual attitude common in France in the 1950s.

Our parents drove Théo crazy. Maman, for instance, loved the cinema, and as Papa had no interest in being shut in a darkened auditorium, she was in the habit of going to light-hearted musicals with her son. Except that, Théo had grown too old to go out with his mother... Nevertheless, he was an affectionate brother, who was willing enough to take me to a film now and then, even if I was still just a child. An example is a matinée performance of Alfred Hitchcock's *To Catch a Thief* with Grace Kelly and Cary Grant. Coming out of the film, Théo said that he'd like to see the next one too, *The Inspector General* with Danny Kaye. I wondered whether this was really a good idea and whether our parents would like the plan, but he cut me short, 'The point is, we've got time to see two films and enough money for a hot-dog.'

My reservations quickly disappeared. I gave in to him. With Théo, I always felt I was in safe hands, and there was never any room for boredom.

At the end of the 1950s, when Théo was eighteen, Papa decided to sell his business in Paris and set up a hairdresser's in La Frette. He had a new salon built in our garden, opening onto the street, between the market square and the station. The launch took place with a great deal of publicity with a grand reception helping to mark the occasion. From then on, word of mouth did the rest; the new hairdressing salon at La Frette was a great success.

That same year, we set off on holiday to Trouville. Théo, who had always been a natural performer and loved to sing, signed up for a variety contest on the beach, taking first prize with his interpretation of songs by Luis Mariano and Frank Sinatra. There is no doubt that this success pushed him to reconsider his future career path, but in no way did he renounce his business studies, knowing how important to his parents they were. When he finished his exams, he even enrolled at a hairdressing college, Chantoiseau School, on rue de Trevise, near the church of Saint-Eugène; and he spent part of his free time helping Papa in the salon.

He was preoccupied though. Being nearly twenty is not easy. You are on the threshold of adulthood you sense the time is coming when you must make your own choices. And, above all, boys of that generation had to face a serious problem: 'events' in Algeria, as they were described at the time. Algeria had gone to war over independence and the fighting was fierce. The youngsters talked about it all the time. Théo, normally so vivacious, became reserved. He often had the blues. And his sadness caused me a great deal of pain. Little by little, I came to understand what was causing it, as I saw Papa paying great attention to each new broadcast on the radio concerning 'the events'. Théo, who was old enough to do his military service, had every chance of being sent there, to North Africa, where many young Frenchmen were being killed. This worry never left him this anxiety about having to do his duty at the front made him see the future as bleak.

As soon as Théo got his driving-licence, Papa loaned him the bottle-green Simca Vedette so he could go for a spin and get used to the traffic. Unfortunately, he had a bump straightaway. This experience left him completely discouraged and when he came home, he said to me, 'I'm not driving again.'

He stuck to his word and from that day on, refused to drive.

Then came the last summer we all spent together. We set off as a family for le Touquet. But this was a depressing holiday. Théo wouldn't speak much, spending most of the time shut in his bedroom. We didn't hear him laugh, or sing, or rehearse Frank Sinatra's songs. Maman used to knock on his door: 'Come with us, Théo! Don't stay on your own like this.'

'Leave him in peace,' Papa would interpose.

Papa didn't say a word. He preferred to suffer in silence and keep to himself the dark threats that recalled sad memories. No doubt he re-lived the moment when his father was beaten by the Turks, conscripted by force into the army. He must have been remembering how he lost his father when he was nine.

Perhaps because they wanted to ward off this prospect, or to try to boost his morale, my parents organised a big celebration for Théo's twentieth birthday. The hairdressing salon was completely redecorated for the occasion. The work-top over the wash-basins was covered with a table cloth to set off an enormous confection by the best pastry-cook in Cormeilles-en-Paris. Alongside it were petits-fours and champagne. With great enthusiasm, I helped in the preparations for the party in honour of my much-loved brother. And I resolved to make myself beautiful, for I was already fourteen years old.

The guests had been invited for 7.30 p.m. I had chosen a pretty dress and wore no socks because it was so hot – Théo's birthday was in January but we were celebrating it that year during the summer, before he was called up for military service. I was not yet allowed to wear stockings, and high heels were even less acceptable. 'Not before you're sixteen!' said my mother. And Papa went even further. 'Not before you're eighteen!' It would be sixteen, decidedly... But that evening, for Théo's twentieth, I settled for my pretty dress and sandals.

At once, I realised that there was not one, but two parties. The first was my parents' gathering, with people their own age and their children – almost the whole village had turned up. The second, which interested me far more, brought together all my brother's friends, young men in formal jackets and ties, and young women in stunning cocktail dresses. People came up to me. I said hello. However, already, the young people were forming lively groups from which rang out bursts of laughter. To them, I was too young. As for Théo, he was far too busy to worry about his little sister! As I didn't want to bother him, or risk being an imposition, I preferred to beat a retreat and join my parents' guests, my young sister, my cousins.

Maman asked me then, 'How's it going over there?'

'The girls are in wonderful dresses.'

'Do they like the sandwiches?'

'I think they're more interested in the champagne.'

'Why don't you stay with them?'

'Because I'm still too young!'

I did appreciate the fact that Théo had let me mix with his friends, even for a little while.

Over the course of the evening, with the help of the champagne, the singing grew louder in both camps. There were even some adults willing to throw themselves into the difficult exercise of Cossack dancing, in other words crouching and kicking their legs out to the sides. Several succeeded in the endeavour without falling and earned loud applause. To my parents' great joy, my brothers' young friends joined us and they too started dancing Russian-style.

Théo's party finished at 5a.m. Not one drop of champagne was left by then. It was the last social gathering before my brother left for Algeria.

3

Barely a few weeks after this much-anticipated birthday party, Théo left to do military service. As the separation drew nearer, the atmosphere in the house became extremely sombre. According to the news broadcast on the radio, the war now stretched across all Algerian territory and ever more French soldiers were being sent into combat. And that one word, 'war', evoked so many bad personal memories for my parents.

I can still see Théo leaving the house with his small suitcase, saying that it wasn't worth taking any clothes because the army would give him a uniform. Maman was mute with grief. My brother was directed towards an army base in a nearby suburb. That same afternoon,he called us on the phone, 'We're going straight to Marseilles. And from Marseilles, it's the boat to Algeria.'

The atmosphere in the hairdressing salon changed from one day to the next. Many clients who came for a hairdo also had sons serving in the army in North Africa, and Papa left the radio on permanently so as not to miss any news bulletins. When the subject was

Algeria, he turned up the sound and all chatter immediately ceased, so that each one of us could listen carefully. Sometimes, Maman would wipe a tear away under her permed hairdo.

Like all the families who had a son over there, we prepared a parcel every day. It was a way to help Théo to cope with his fate, in his garrison in Aïn Safra. It was also a way for us to think about him, to be at his side, to prevent us from being overcome by the void he had left. My brother received so much food that he had enough and more to spare, even sharing it with his friends. However, as he told us in his letters, there was a problem with the water: the enemy was contaminating the reservoirs and men were falling sick. This news shocked Papa, reminding him of his own father, dead of dysentery for the same reason: poisoned water. He decided to send money to Théo, as well as parcels, so he could buy something to drink for his less fortunate companions.

Still very young, I found it hard to imagine the experiences of the soldiers in the Atlas Mountains which were so horrific that it was even difficult to speak about them. But I had a strong urge to put my own hand to the wheel and join in with the attempt to improve the basics of my brother's daily life. On my own initiative, I decided one day to make up a parcel for him. And, as I wanted to be as nice as possible, I put in one pot of jam, two packets of crackers, and one slab of butter. That would be just perfect for him to have a proper breakfast. Some time later, a letter from Théo mentioned the parcel, 'Thank Chrissy, but it was really hot and the items arrived all melted together; the biscuits were crushed, the butter had melted and the pot of jam had smashed.' My parents were surprised to read these words. They had no idea that I had taken it upon myself to send Théo a parcel just from me.

'Next time, send him tinned food,' Papa told me, 'not perishables.'

Maman, who worked very rarely at the salon in those days, was always anxious waiting for the postman. When she saw him, she glanced his way with a little, nervous smile. Papa, for his part, dropped whatever he was doing, and ran to meet him. The postman understood, as he was used to it. We weren't the only family to have a son in Algeria. Having said that, we were spoiled when it came to mail. Théo wrote regularly. Sometimes, we didn't get a letter for several days but then two or three would come at the same time. He never spoke to us about the political situation, never alluded to the risks he was facing. He kept to descriptions of his friends, of the parcels he'd received and the beautiful landscapes in which his operations took place. Behind these topics, intended to reassure us, we could nevertheless sense the overshadowing menace, for the radio often mentioned 'incidents' in the course of which several soldiers had been killed. Deep inside, each of us wondered, 'What if that happened to Théo?' But we were careful to keep such thoughts to ourselves.

At the end of several months, Théo let us know he had a pass to come to Paris and sit his diploma as a hairdresser. However, our hopes were soon dashed. He arrived on a plane, took his exam and went off again straight away. He wasn't allowed to come to the house to see us, not even for a few minutes. My parents had difficulty even crossing his path at the Chantoiseau School. For all that, this brief episode was to mark an important step because on his return to Aïn Safra, my brother took on the rôle of secretary to the commander, a post he held until his demobilisation and return to France. He was even offered promotion, with a view to becoming an officer at a later stage, but he turned it down. The least one could say was that Théo lacked any military tendencies. He was a born entertainer, a dreamer, a pacifist. He accepted that he had to do his duty, as did all his comrades – but to take up a command was something he'd have found impossible.

Théo stayed for thirty-three months in Algeria nearly three years of his life passing in military service, day after day another brush with danger. The last few months were the hardest, for him as well as for us. My brother was waiting for his demobilisation, without ever getting a precise date for his return to France. He wrote to us that each time a final payday was fixed, some event took place and everything was thrown up in the air again. Truly agonising. In the end, he stopped telling us when he'd be back, so he wouldn't have to contradict himself, letting us down after all that wait. He was so successful that we had the surprise of our lives to see him appear one fine day over the garden gate. He was still holding his small suitcase and was wearing a lovely suede jacket – in those days a very trendy item of clothing. But his shoulders were swimming in it, he'd lost so much weight! Inevitably, his arrival opened the floodgates for tears of joy and hugs. Papa and Maman were overcome with emotion. Maman wanted to make something for her son to eat, straight away. We simply stood there, looking at each other. We didn't know what to say. Besides, there was nothing we could say. News, anecdotes, projects for the future, all that would come later. For the moment, we just wanted to make the most of our happiness. My brother had returned to La Frette, my parents were at peace. At last we could live without that sword of Damocles hanging over our heads.

Still, it wasn't long before I realised that the war had left its mark on Théo. Always so light-hearted, he seemed taciturn nowadays. When we were in Paris, he seemed lost. One might say he was trying to find his bearings. Or that he was always on his guard. Before Algeria, Théo was a high-spirited boy, in a hurry, who would cross the road darting between vehicles. Now, he would hesitate, wait for several long minutes before setting out. At first, I understood his reactions; a man who had just spent three years in the desert inevitably had to readjust to the racket and bustle of the city. Anyway, he said himself, 'You know, Christie, the desert is vast silence.'

But it was not just about the desert. It was also about fear, about having to be constantly on the defensive, the fact that he'd lived with the stress of the threat of permanent danger, often invisible, but capable of surging up at any moment and carrying everything with it. Then, much later, Théo revealed that he had seen many of his companions die. He told me about men being sent on duty, into ambushes that killed them, about vehicles blown up by mines, of a soldier who'd taken his place one night and been killed.

When I listened to Théo conjure up this sort of memory, I could see the signs of suffering etched on his face. For him, speaking of such things meant re-opening deep wounds. I realised that he needed time to readjust to our life. These days it seems to me that Théo's character gained its 'tragic' side at this time, a troubled spirit who seemed to attract crises and who would later find this echoed in the personality of Piaf.

Whatever the case, our life had changed. At seventeen, I too was enrolled in the Chantoiseau School of hairdressing. I remember that sometimes Théo came to wait for me outside the image of a beautiful, melancholy young man. My classmates were envious and eaten up by curiosity. I could hear them whispering together.

'Have you seen Christie, that boyfriend she has?'

'You think it's her boyfriend?'

One of them, unable to hold back any longer, expressed her feelings. 'He is just gorgeous!'

'But he's my brother!'

She wasn't convinced...

After hairdressing school, I in turn entered the family business in my turn. For a while, we all worked together, Papa, Théo, three employees and me. And Maman came to the rescue when we couldn't cope. Days flew by, punctuated by gales of laughter.

But my brother soon made it clear that he needed his independence. He was a little bored at La Frette, felt constrained by our small world, our warm nest. He started to spend evenings on the Left Bank. It was Saint-Germain-des-Prés' finest hour, the time of

Jacques Prévert, Boris Vian, Juliette Gréco and Mouloudji. The jazz clubs were bouncing and the youth had discovered bebop. Variety artists had a huge influence on young people who were trying to find themselves. Entertainers and writers too. Authors, actors, painters, journalists everyone gathered on the rue de Rennes, between Montparnasse and the Saint-Germain crossroads, where Jean-Paul Sartre was expounding his pessimistic philosophy which, curiously enough, was a perfect match with what had become of Théo since his return from Algeria: an attractive youth, full of charm, but who, in reaching adulthood, had contemplated the dark and random nature of his existence.

Théo was in Paris every day, spending time with new friends and coming home very late at night. Papa did not look kindly on this change in behaviour. When he reproached my brother, Théo replied that his life had been on hold for three years and he needed some fun now. At other times, he said he wanted to go to the United States.

'There are days,' he said, 'when even the Left Bank bores me.'

Disenchanted, he didn't get involved with his girlfriends. Besides, he didn't try to seduce them it was often the girls who came after him. At first, he just let things happen, he accepted playing the game. Then he found it tedious so he moved on to the next one.

When he stayed at La Frette to get some rest, he read a great deal: Tolstoy, Dostoyevsky. The two employees in our community bookshop went into ecstasies when they saw Théo and he enjoyed spending money there. I think he regretted the fact that circumstances had prevented him from studying literature. Certainly, the milieu in which he felt most at ease was exactly that bizarre mix of writers and creative artists who he enjoyed meeting each evening.

One day, a new friend offered him a job at the Elizabeth Arden hairdressing salon. The friend was an American who, from before the war, had been demonstrating to women how to apply make-up. This was a prestigious salon, opening up the possibility of a career in the United States.

'There is one post available,' said the friend. 'Are you interested?'

Théo made an appearance straightaway at the place Vendôme and was given an interview, at the end of which he was hired! That same evening, he announced the news to us.

'I'm going to leave La Frette. I'm going to set myself up in Paris.'

Papa couldn't hide his disappointment. He had always imagined that Théo would carry on the business. It was even a source of tension between them for Théo had never felt it was his vocation to become a hairdresser. His talent, his character and his imagination all directed him towards the arts, performance, variety shows. If he had agreed to study business, it was out of filial duty, from family loyalty, to make my parents' old dream come true. But he didn't see himself making the sacrifice as far as settling at La Frette was concerned. He explained to us that Elizabeth Arden offered an acceptable compromise; this way of earning a living – and even of earning it very well – would also allow him to see his arty friends and go to the Left Bank.

My parents often told me that the only subject to arouse tension between them was their children. So far as Théo was concerned, this tension was at its height. For them, the situation had reached the point of pulling them apart. There was no actual hostility in the relationship with their son: their mutual love remained intact. But Théo was determined not to give in. He was fully an adult by then. He had lived through painful experiences, which had marked him forever. Back from Algeria, depressed, he needed to run wild. Writing these lines, I can't help but think of 'La Foule', the song by Edith which expresses so well how Théo felt at that time.

Je revois la ville en fête et délire
Suffoquant sous le soleil et sous la joie
Et j'entends dans la musique les cris, les rires
Qui éclatent et rebondissent autour de moi...

(I see the city again, its parties and excitement, but
I suffocate beneath the sun, beneath the joy
And I hear cries in the music, the laughter
That rings out and echoes all round me.)

My parents offered him a comfortable provincial existence when all the while he aspired to something different.

Nevertheless, he waited two more years before moving out. He left every day for work at Elizabeth Arden and came home to sleep at La Frette, but when his night life was all-consuming – and it was often all-consuming – he would stay over at a friend's. Or at a girlfriend's for he was a big hit with women without ever becoming attached to any of them. My feeling is that he needed to love someone, but the scars left by the war would take time to heal. They kept him suspended in a state of mind somewhere between anxiety and the desire to have fun.

'They're looking for a hairdresser for Elizabeth Arden in New York. They've asked for my C.V.'

Papa didn't know how to react, nor Maman.

As for me, I was eighteen and, for me too, it was not unknown for me to head out with friends, to go to 'rave-ups' to use the term of the time, or to night-clubs. We drank coca-cola, put our hips out doing the twist, the latest fad from the United States, and we watched boys. Sometimes, I would be late home. Maman knew. She wasn't supposed to tell Papa, who would have been annoyed. These sneaky nocturnal homecomings had something extraordinary about them. I shared a bedroom with my young sister, who, of course, couldn't get to sleep until I was back. I used to approach the house on tiptoes and I'd throw gravel at the window. My sister would come downstairs and open the door for me. I'd whisper, 'Papa's asleep?'

'Yes.'

I'd climb the stairs quickly and slip under the sheets fully dressed, without even taking my shoes off. I'd pull the coverlet right over my head and feign sleep, still high on the atmosphere of the club, the music, the twist and the smoke. After a minute, I would hear the door open gently, then Papa saying to Maman, 'She's back, she's sleeping.'

Proof that, in fact, Maman couldn't bring herself to hide the truth from him. There was an agreement between them. She would pretend to be the only one who knew, and he would hang on to his image as the father, the boss, the harsh guardian. Except that we weren't exactly 'children'...

Did Papa think I went out too much? Did he want to protect me against certain misadventures that could happen to young girls? He informed me that I would shortly be going on a journey with my mother. 'You'll be going to Egypt for two or three weeks.'

I had family over there in the form of an uncle, an aunt and their children, my cousins.

I was over the moon with this prospect. It would be my first long journey! Of course, I had no idea how many other journeys were in store for me...

We took a night train that linked Paris to Venice. My brief experience of Venice was like an enchantment, a dream come to life. Then we embarked on the *Achilleos*, a cruise ship belonging to Aristotle Onassis. After one stop at Piraeus, we headed directly for Alexandria.

The city was so noisy that it shocked me. The moment that we arrived, a horde of men rushed on board by hanging from the ropes, before the gangplank even touched the quayside, where a dense crowd lay in wait for us. Trying to raise her voice above the din, Maman said, 'Look, there's your uncle, my brother-in-law!'

A man in a light-coloured suit was waving at us.

'He's got grey hair already,' Maman observed, taken aback. She hadn't seen him for ten years.

It was the first time that I'd met the family members who lived in Egypt. Since President Nasser came to power, this country no longer looked kindly on Europeans. Many had already left, and others would soon follow, including my uncle, my aunt and their children, who set up home in Athens shortly thereafter. The ordinary people, however, were very welcoming and hospitable. I remember the women, in particular, taking my hand in the street as a show of affection.

My cousins took us to see Farouk's Palace, the pyramids and the Cairo museums. I still remember the mummies, stripped of their bandages their red hair, their hands, their nails. It is one thing to study Egypt in school but quite another to see with your own eyes these beings who seem to have travelled through time. What were they trying to tell us? It was fascinating and frightening at the same time.

After these visits, Maman would often receive an invitation card, in a white envelope, virginal. One evening we attended one of the dos for Europeans, which would sometimes finish at dawn with a cruise along the Nile. The next day, a Greek youth turned up at the door and said to my mother, 'I would like to speak to you on a serious matter.'

He had come to give an account of himself in person… to make a marriage proposal! Egyptian Greeks kept up this tradition. Maman took all this in with a smile sending an affectionate look in my direction. As far as I was concerned, I was petrified at the idea of marrying a man with whom I'd barely spent two hours, which is why I preferred to say nothing, even if I was supposedly the one most concerned.

The trip finished with a stay in Athens. It was mind-blowing to see the land of my ancestors at last, and the amazing light that played on the Acropolis. The music of the language, above all, charmed me. Not to mention the cuisine, exactly like Yaya's and Maman's.

On our return to La Frette, things had not changed and would stay the same all that year. Days all followed the same routine and we were preoccupied with the same questions.

That was when Théo received a letter from New York. He'd been accepted at Elizabeth Arden. We were all together in the salon when he unfolded the letter to show it to Papa.

'Do you really want to move house to the United States?' sighed Papa, passing the letter to Maman.

She was still very sun-tanned after our long trip and yet literally shivered at the idea of soon living apart from her son, separated by a vast ocean!

'It's what I wanted,' Théo replied.

A flicker of hope ran across the salon. I interposed, 'You wanted it but now you don't? Is that it?'

'Yes, that's it.'

'Why is that?' Papa asked, forcing himself to hide the relief he felt.

'Because.'

The house adjusted to this mystery. Why had Théo changed his mind? Théo, who always said he was bored in France, who spoke of nothing but leaving, who had waited so impatiently, or so it had seemed, for the reply from Elizabeth Arden! Now he had it, his letter. He'd been offered a job with one of the most prestigious hairdressing salons on the planet. And lo and behold, he'd decided to stay in Paris...

Everyone was stupefied, but neither Papa, nor Maman, nor I dared to bring the subject out into the open again, for fear that Théo would change his mind one more time.

Two or three days later, when I was alone in the back room of the hairdressing salon, Théo came in saying, 'See that telephone, Christie? At 6 p.m. in a few minutes, it's going to ring. And do you know who'll be at the other end of the line?'

I waited because he was looking at me with such intensity.

'Edith Piaf.'

4

Théo had met Piaf through the intermediary of one of his Left Bank friends, Claude Figus, a singer who would later die in mysterious circumstances. The evening was spent among other young people, music-lovers with whom Théo often enjoyed himself. They danced, they talked their heads off, heads spinning a little; they had a drink, which called for another drink, and so it went on. All at once, Théo noticed that he was too late for the last train for La Frette. Figus said to him, 'Too late to go home to bed, old man. It's now or never to meet Edith. How's about it? What do you think?'

Théo admired Claude Figus. He knew the other man was close to the singer and held the position of her secretary. This slim man with curly hair had worshipped Piaf since adolescence, had frequented the theatres where she appeared, had hidden in the wings in the hope of crossing his idol's path. In the end, he found a place in her life: he was like her shadow.

'Meet Edith Piaf!' Théo exclaimed. 'You know that's my dream. But at this time of night! She'll be asleep, won't she?'

'Edith never goes to sleep before five in the morning. And she always needs a lot of people around her. I'll call her and tell her I'm on my way with a friend. Is that O.K.?'

Claude rang her from a phone booth.

'No problem, Théo. Let's go.'

My brother could not believe his ears. 'What did you tell her?'

'That you'd missed the last train. Don't be so shy!'

Théo, in general, wasn't shy at all. He was an attractive young man, with great presence and a classic taste in clothes. He had an aristocratic beauty of which Maman was very proud, and which was apparently passed down to him by his paternal grandfather. To which was added another attraction French-style elegance. He was also used to meeting all sorts of people in the clubs of Saint-Germain-des-Prés, where celebrities from the worlds of art, literature and variety mingled every evening in the crowd of strangers. But that particular night he found himself in what was, to say the least, an unexpected situation. He'd been sure that Claude Figus would present him to Edith sooner or later. But to turn up at her home like that, in the middle of the night...

The two friends jumped into a taxi and headed for the 15th arrondissement.

'You'll see,' said Claude, 'there are lots of tasty nibbles. It's very laid-back and we eat in the kitchen.'

This was the 20th January, 1962. My brother Théo and his friend Claude Figus had just got out of the car in front of 67 bis, boulevard Lannes. They were right next to the Bois de Boulogne. The racecourse at

Auteuil was lit up in patches. Théo lifted his eyes up to the apartment block.

'She lives on the ground floor,' Claude clarified.

The two friends passed through a wrought-iron porch and went forward into the pale marble lobby. The floor was covered with a red carpet. Claude rang the bell at the door, which opened to reveal a young, carefree woman, a hank of hair falling in front of her eyes. This was Christiane, daughter of Suzanne, the cook.

'Come on in. Madame is resting. But she'll be along.'

Claude and Théo entered the lounge, where a black piano was enthroned. At the back were two petrol-blue armchairs, a settee, a low table littered with sheet music. One of the armchairs was occupied by Jacques Plante who was in the act of editing song lyrics only recently sprung from his pen. His career had begun in the middle of the occupation and he was by this time a successful songwriter. The wider public, even though ignorant of his name, knew the songs he'd written for André Claveau, Yves Montand, Georges Guétary and Line Renaud. He'd only been working with Piaf for a short while, Edith Piaf who until then had been the missing jewel in his crown.

Claude Figus took on the introductions. Théo sat down on the edge of the divan. At two in the morning, the door opened and Edith appeared, wearing a pale blue dressing-gown, so slight and frail in that enormous room. Seeing Théo, she asked, 'Are you the one who missed your train?'

Piaf seemed from the start to be struck by my brother's good looks. She found him to be good company. She kept her blue-eyed gaze on him. She gently interrogated him. Théo told her that he worked for Elizabeth Arden. Realising he felt shy, Edith turned to Planque, switching to that teasing note which had made her so famous, 'So, Jacques? Is the song finished then?'

During the discussion that followed, Edith often sought to catch my brother's eye. He remained silent but ate up every word uttered. No doubt his intuition whispered in his ear that perhaps this was a turning-point in his life. At one point, Edith demanded, 'What's your star sign?'

Théo was Aquarius. Straight away Piaf disappeared only to return after a few minutes with a little book by André Barbeau, a well-known astrologer at that time. She opened it, read a passage. Then she said to Théo, quoting Barbeau, 'Aquarians are reserved with strangers. But once you earn their trust, they open up.'

Two days later, Théo received a call from Claude.

'She liked you. She wants to see you again. Tonight even.' Talking to Figus, she had let slip some of her thoughts about Théo. 'Has your friend lost his tongue? Is he as smart as he's good-looking?'

That same evening, my brother went to dinner at boulevard Lannes. In the kitchen sat round the table, were Jacques Plante, Bernard Dimey and Francis Lai. Dimey, a poet in love with Montmartre, used to offer his song lyrics to the great entertainers of that era: Juliette Gréco, Charles Aznavour and Patachou, to cite but a few. As for Francis Lai, everyone remembers the film themes and soundtracks he wrote. He too had only known Piaf for a few days and came over as quite reserved.

But Piaf, who had dined with Brigitte Bardot the previous night, kept the conversation sparkling. Wearing the same pale blue dressing-gown, she gave her impressions of 'B.B.' 'An amazing girl. Funny as anything. Pretty as a picture. But, above all, she is *genuine*.'

To be genuine; this was the highest compliment that Edith ever conferred. She turned to Francis Lai. 'You have some new melodies for me?'

'Not really. Nothing special, Edith,' replied Francis, who had a timid side.

'Let's see how it goes, all the same.'

Francis got up to fetch his accordion. He launched into several numbers. Then Piaf suddenly said to him, using the familiar 'tu' form. 'Play that one again for me.' When Piaf started calling you 'tu', it meant you'd been accepted. Francis played it one more time. Piaf hummed along. The alchemy started working. Théo could not believe his eyes; he was witnessing the birth of a song that would be sung, perhaps very soon, by one of the world's greatest music-hall stars.

Piaf was extremely tired at that time. Three years earlier, she'd had a car accident during a trip with Georges Moustaki, the singer who had written one of her most famous songs, *Milord*. Following the experience, she was hospitalised in Meudon, then at the American hospital in Neuilly. Despite a series of residences in the countryside, she could never really find any peace. Her liver was in a very bad way. Nevertheless, she carried on working, like people cling to a lifeline. And she had never given up on love. Anyway, she was encouraged in this by André Barbeau, the astrologer, with whom she stayed in contact, and who'd promised her she'd meet someone. Barbeau had predicted that 'Love will come into your life. A man younger than you. And who will make you very happy.' Piaf was extremely superstitious. At the end of 1961, she saw Barbeau again and he confirmed his prediction. And now, here was this tall young man, with dark brown hair and a melancholy look, a twenty-six year old dreamer who'd turned up on her doorstep. That evening, during the dinner that marked their second encounter, Piaf's edginess spread to everyone else, and the driver, who was serving upset the sauce onto the tablecloth, then dropped a glass, and then, while trying to right it, pulled all the place settings onto the floor. Edith's reaction? A gale of laughter!

She was like that, especially in this period. She would switch abruptly from one mood to another. She was capable of almost fainting from nerves one minute and then laughing herself silly the next. It's true that she lived on a knife-edge, forced to be careful at every instant. Everything she did was monitored quantities of food, doses of medication, the temperature of the apartment. She didn't even know whether she should be singing, whether the effort might kill her. The doctors forbade her even one drop of alcohol.

In the days that followed, Théo got into the habit of going to boulevard Lannes, at Edith's invitation. Once again, there were incidents with the tablecloth

Edith mimed a dramatic fainting scene and clutched the tablecloth, which she pulled suddenly. Everything fell upside down. Théo and the other guests ended up pulling from their side to avoid further damage. When she understood their strategy, Piaf rose with a dignified air, left the dining-room and headed for the lounge. After a short pause, her guests rejoined her, and, doubled up with laughter, she accused them, 'You had me there, you bastards!'

There was always a crowd in the apartment and never enough chairs for all of the visitors. Théo, a regular these days, sat on the floor and listened to what was going on. Edith trying to sing. Edith seized with anxiety. Edith complaining about the heat. Complaining about the cold. Demanding that someone open the windows, at the risk of catching pneumonia. Taking her pills. Giving in to despair and ranting to her friends. 'It's over! I will never go on stage again! You're just sugaring the pill for me!'

Théo came to share the huge concerns about Edith that ruled her household. One evening when he arrived at boulevard Lannes, he found a heavy atmosphere in the apartment. Edith wasn't in the lounge. She wasn't in the kitchen either.

'Is she resting in her room?'

Louis Barrier, the singer's agent, approached him, whispering. 'She's really not well. She should go to hospital but she won't hear of it. Perhaps you could try and convince her. She says she trusts you.'

Very surprised to hear that he might have some influence on Piaf, Théo went and knocked softly on her door. He found her in her bed, shivering, buried under the covers while the window was wide open. But Edith brightened when she recognised him.

'They want to put me in a clinic. For bronchitis! Are they crazy or what?'

Perhaps it was bronchitis, thought Théo, but bronchitis was enough to take her from them, given the feeble state she'd been in for months! Edith stared at him from above the sheet, breathing with difficulty. Théo felt that this little woman, exhausted and shaking, cowering in fear, was only waiting for some reassurance from him. He leaned towards her.

'You've got to be sensible. It's only a matter of a few days. You'll feel much better afterwards.'

That same day, she was transported to the Ambroise-Paré Clinic in Neuilly. In his turn, Figus set off for the apartment in a blind panic, at the stage when the ambulance was already en route. Louis Barrier was in the act of giving out instructions, 'Absolute discretion. No-one must know!'

Louis, Claude and Théo accompanied Edith to Ambroise-Paré, where the doctors diagnosed bronchopneumonia. Their prognosis was guarded; they didn't want to commit themselves for another two days.

That evening, Théo went back to La Frette, depressed. At once, he was bombarded with questions.

'What's happened?'

'It's Edith.'

'She's ill.'

Is it serious?'

'Yes.'

Refusing to say another word, he went upstairs and shut himself in his room.

I understood that from this time on Piaf would occupy a huge place in my brother's life.

5

The next day, Théo rushed over to Ambroise-Paré, where the patient had been put in an oxygen tent. Pushing open the door of her room, he saw Edith at once make a sign that he should approach her. She was extremely pale. By gestures, she asked him to pop his head under the tent because she was too frail to raise her voice. Théo complied and Edith murmured sadly, in one breath, 'I'm camping, you know…'

While Théo held her hand to warm it up and give her the courage to go on, she added, 'I was right to keep the window open. I knew I needed air. Here's the proof!'

'I brought you something.'

The delicate pallor of her little face brightened with surprise.

Théo pulled a little *evzone* out of his pocket, a soldier from the Greek guard, wearing his coloured uniform. 'For you.'

Edith was moved, touched. She forced a weak smile, then a genuine laugh.

Two days later, the patient had recovered her energy and colour. There was no longer a need for the oxygen tent. The doctor had even been obliged to reprimand a nurse to whom Piaf had given an improvised performance based on *Bel Indifférent*, the play that Jean Cocteau had written for her. Generally speaking, the doctors demanded absolute calm around their patient. But it was a lost cause. As soon as she was feeling better, she radiated warm humanity. And she received a constant stream of visitors. Surrounded by her court, she launched into new projects. My brother was amazed at this renewed vitality. Later, Edith told him, with a mysterious air, 'We need to talk. As soon as I'm home again.'

The next day, back at the clinic, Théo found her in a bad mood, sitting on the edge of her bed.

'They won't let me out.'

As he had done several days earlier, Théo gently advised her to keep being sensible, because she could see the results.

Shortly afterwards, the others turned up Francis Lai, Claude Figus and Louis Barrier, whom everyone called 'Loulou'. In an instant, the room was full of people. Piaf suddenly had an idea. 'Francis, is your instrument in the car?' While Francis went out to get his accordion, she added, 'We'll show them whether or not I'm cured and on top form!'

A while later, the Ambroise-Paré Clinic was reverberating with the chords of *Emporte-moi*, a song sprung from Francis' very own pen. Other snippets followed and the concert lasted all evening, despite the efforts of the doctors and nurses to restore a modicum of calm. Edith was singing from her bed, with Claude Figus on one side, in a suit, and, on the other, my brother, Théo, in a black polo-neck and a suede jacket.

In spite of Loulou's guidelines, word had spread that Piaf had been hospitalised in a clinic at Neuilly. And as Neuilly was packed with clinics, many receptionists faced journalists turning up, some of whom cottoned on quickly to the truth. This explained why knocking could often be heard on the door of Piaf's room – in truth, there was so much noise that it was only possible to hear the knocking during an interval between songs... To those reporters who succeeded in getting into her room, Piaf introduced my brother, declaring, 'This is Théo. He is going to be my second secretary. He will take care of my mail. Claude will deal with my diary. See, boys, how well organised I am. And it's not over yet!'

When she turned to Théo, her eyes were full of hope and passionate love. On that note, she burst out laughing.

And the next day, it was Théo she called to ask whether he could collect her from the clinic. 'I'm coming out today.'

Except the entrance to the building was occupied by a pack of reporters! Loulou didn't want them to take photos of Edith, because her face was still swollen after several days of treatment.

'We need to find a private exit,' he said.

Théo and Edith thus left the hospital by a service door. Unfortunately, two photographers were hiding at the back of the building and the images appeared in the press, with Piaf looking ill.

At boulevard Lannes, Suzanne and her daughter Christiane were in charge of preparing Edith's room and making her bed. Piaf arrived back on Théo's arm – tiny, unsteady, weakened but blossoming in the company of this tall young man who'd been thrust into the position of her 'new secretary'. Her band of friends soon followed; in the flash of an eye, the apartment was swarming with people. Realising that they all expected her to go straight to her bedroom, Piaf exclaimed, 'I didn't get out of that clinic just to go back to bed at home! We've got work to do! But first, a cup of tea.'

She used to drink twenty to twenty-five cups a day…

While Suzanne was busy making tea, Piaf drew my brother aside and had a quiet word in his ear. 'These last few days, I've had time to think, you know. I like you very much. I want to do something for you. Don't tell me you intend to curl hair all your life. Really?'

Théo was caught off guard. First there was the business of 'the secretary' in front of the journalists, and now this desire to help him *be* somebody…

Edith continued. 'Claude told me that you were a singer. Is that true?'

Théo preferred to be modest. 'I have sung a little. Sinatra, Luis Mariano. I once won a talent contest on the radio, at Trouville. Nothing important.'

'Well then, show me what you can do. That way, I'll know what you're really made of. Do you want to think about it?'

It wasn't through a sense of vocation that Théo had started curling hair, but to make our parents happy

Papa especially, as he was the one who had always hoped Théo would take over the family business. In reality, Théo felt that he'd always been full of artistic ambitions. He loved literature, cinema and music-hall with a passion. If he'd been able to hold himself together in Algeria, it was largely due to his books and his record-player – particularly one disc, which he knew by heart, *L'Hymne à l'amour*:

Le ciel bleu sur nous peut s'effondrer
Et la terre peut bien s'écrouler
Peu m'importes si tu m'aimes
Je me fous du monde entier.

(Let the blue sky fall on us
The earth quake under us
I don't care so long as you love me
The rest of the world can go hang.)

Circumstances had dictated that it was his friend Figus who opened the door to this universe that fascinated him. Wasn't now the moment to seize this chance which would probably never occur again?

'I've already thought about it, Edith. Thank you…'

'Think about it again, all the same. I'll give you until tomorrow.'

To please Edith, Théo replied that he would reflect on the matter in peace and quiet, but when he left boulevard Lannes that evening, his decision was already made. He knew that only one ordeal was in store: announcing the news to our family informing Papa and Maman of his choice…

At La Frette, we dined together again. At first, we were content to have Théo with us. Then we felt that something was about to happen, he seemed so preoccupied. Over dessert, he told us quite simply, 'I'm giving up hairdressing. I'm going to give singing a shot.'

Théo's statement was made without any aggression but his tone allowed no contradiction. A heavy silence descended. Then Papa reacted, predictably.

'You have a good job and you want to throw everything up in the air to be a singer?'

'This way of life doesn't suit me,' Théo replied.

'You know how hard I've worked to create this salon, to make the business flourish. A business I intended to go to my children!'

'Everyone has to find his own way, Papa. We are different, you and I. Our lives are different. Our reactions, too. You arrived here from Turkey at seventeen, I grew up in France. Our characters are different, in any case… '

'It's not a question of character, but of common sense!' replied Papa, who was fighting hard not to give in to his anger. 'I'm not speaking for my sake but for yours. I don't want my son to make a big mistake! Variety artist! Do you really think that's a decent way of life?'

'I'm not a child any more, Papa. I've been to war in Algeria. After what I saw over there, I think I'm capable of deciding for myself what purpose I want to give my life.'

Maman said nothing. Neither did I. We found it really difficult to bear the argument between Papa and Théo. Family life is so sweet when there is harmony between parents and children, between brothers and sisters! But my mother and I had realised that the shadow of Piaf was floating in our dining-room, that it was as if she hovered there above us, like a symbol of destiny. Besides, everyone could tell to the extent of Théo's resolve. He hadn't brought up the matter to hear his parents' opinions but to inform them of a decision already firmly rooted inside him, about which nothing could make him change his mind.

It was Maman who finally broke the silence, concluding, 'When do you leave?'

Théo shrugged his shoulders, with an apologetic expression. 'Soon.'

The next day at boulevard Lannes, Edith was waiting for him. 'Well? Have you thought about it?'

'Yes, I want to go for it.'

'And your parents?'

'They're not keen. The arty crowd worries them.'

'Introduce me to them. They'll see that I don't intend to eat you alive.'

And Edith added, without ceremony, 'Well, when are you going to come over?'

'As soon as possible. After enough time to help my father get organised.'

Fifteen days later, Théo left the hairdressing salon. Piaf welcomed him into the kitchen, saying, 'Get a cup of tea and let's get to work!'

'The mail?'

He hadn't forgotten that she'd planned to make him her second secretary.

'No, leave the mail to Claude. Sing me something instead.'

Théo hadn't rehearsed anything, no song was prepared. Above all, he was intimidated at the idea of singing in front of Piaf. Seeing his embarrassment, she continued, laughing, 'Francis is here. Just in the other room. Go and tell him to teach you a song. I'll come back in a while and listen to how it's going.'

She had already chosen the number by Francis Lai which would form the content of Théo's audition... The lyrics were by Bernard Dimey. Francis, Figus and Théo worked on the song for two hours. Then they taped it. Edith reappeared in the lounge.

'Well?'

'I haven't got the nerve to sing for you,' said my brother, 'but I can play it back for you.'

'Why can't you sing for me? Do I scare you?'

'It's not that but...'

Piaf never liked to let something go. 'If you sing for an audience one day, what are you going to do? Are you going to ask them if they want to hear a tape?'

Théo looked at Francis and Claude, embarrassed. In any case, the recording was not very good and he knew that. In the end, he decided to sing the number live for Edith, who listened attentively. Afterwards, she delivered her verdict. 'He has a lovely voice. I will launch his career.'

6

From the month of March in that year, 1962, Edith' health began to improve. The doctors had stopped the cortisone treatment and the singer's face had regained some bloom. Morale also seemed to be better. Théo and the others had the pleasure of seeing that when she made her appearance in the lounge she no longer wore the inevitable pale blue dressing-gown. From now on, she felt the desire to smarten up she bought trousers and black pullovers, she had her hairdresser call at the house.

You could have said that her horizon had suddenly brightened. At a gathering of her friends, she announced her decision to go on tour that summer. Loulou Barrier gave the impression that he favoured the idea. A programme had to be prepared even though doing so in three months was a tall order, especially for someone just recovering from bronchopneumonia. Besides, as Edith was the first to recognize, 'Three months is not long, boys, we need to get cracking.'

For all that, she had already envisaged her spectacle.

'Théo, you'll be a special guest, with three songs.'

Shocked, Théo had no time to express his surprise. Edith was already continuing, to the whole group, 'Claude will close the first half, with six or seven numbers.'

Figus, moved to tears, threw himself into Edith's arms, 'Am I dreaming or what?'

At that time, he was singing each night in Montmartre at Patachou's, the temple of French *chanson*, where numerous artists had already spread their wings and taken flight – Brassens, Hugues Aufray, Guy Béart, to mention but a few. Edith could not have given him a more fantastic present than this invitation to feature on the same billing as her!

There was general astonishment. Théo already felt overwhelmed. Figus was trying to control his emotions. And Edith was laughing, as if galvanised into action by the sight of their stunned faces. She added, 'As for me, I need material. That's where you come in, Francis.'

All that remained was to get organised. Piaf had already thought about the working arrangements in the apartment for her entourage, given the scale of the project. Claude Figus inherited the room which had previously belonged to Charles Aznavour. On the nights he didn't go back to La Frette, Théo used to sleep on the divan in the library. With regard to rehearsals, Edith would work in one room with her pianist and Figus would be installed in another with Noël Commaret, the pianist who accompanied his sets at Patachou's, and whose name would later be found on my own songs when I became a singer. Yet that time was still to come... As for Jacques Plante, he would shut himself in the kitchen to write his compositions. And, finally, Théo would have the use of the library to rehearse with Francis.

In a few days, the apartment became a real hive of activity where, simultaneously, you could hear three voices, two pianos and an accordion. Not to mention the comments from Loulou Barrier, the discussions, the banter of the usual crowd, and Susan, the cook, calling everyone when a meal was ready... The occupants of neighbouring flats used to tap on the air vents to protest against what they perceived as an unbearable cacophony. Some of them threw buckets of water out of their windows over the musicians as they arrived. But it was not Piaf's style to beat a retreat when faced with adversity; the neighbours, seeing that their complaints and moans were having no effect, ended up making the best of a bad job.

Théo now realised the huge amount of work required to set up such a tour and it terrified him. Nevertheless, he was aware of the chance he'd been given to learn his new career. And as he was to confide in me later, he retained everything he was capable of learning, from his own rehearsals of course, but even more so from observing Piaf. She didn't hesitate to interrupt her own work sessions to come to his aid, to advise him, to encourage him. One day, she sat down beside him on the divan 'Try singing *Pense à moi.*

They were all together in the big lounge and Claude was rehearsing with Francis. Piaf had been present at the end of the session, commenting more and more. And now, as if on a whim, she was asking Théo to interpret a number in Figus's repertoire!

'But... it's Claude's song!'

Pense à moi was not just his song but even Claude's lucky number. It was a powerful melody, long, demanding, almost iconic, the fruit of Bernard Dimey and Francis Lai's talent. Figus performed it each night at Patachou's and it was his most popular song.

'I know it's one of Claude's songs,' Piaf responded impatiently. 'But it's not the right song for him. Whereas it suits you perfectly. Besides, the two of us have spoken about it haven't we, Claude?'

Claude didn't dare contradict Edith; all the same, he was not happy and his resentment showed in his face. Judging that the affair was closed, Piaf turned once more to Théo, insisting, 'Try it, I'm telling you.'

Théo sang it unwillingly. He performed the number once, twice, five times, ten times.

'It's coming,' said Piaf.

Théo was exhausted. 'I can't go on…'

'Yes you can. Continue.' She even showed him how he should move about the stage.

'More expansive in gestures. Occupy the space.'

She possessed this capacity to see the talent in others. And she already saw Théo the way he would be one day. The way he wasn't yet able to see himself an amazing singer, dressed in black, opening his big arms wide, as if to embrace the public, embrace life itself, in that mixture of charm and vulnerability which would become his hallmark.

Pense à moi dans tes prières
Si jamais je meurs demain

(Think of me in your prayers
If I should die tomorrow)

It was a relief when Edith, finally, gave her verdict, 'That's close to sounding good now. I'm happy. Next, a cup of tea! That will relax you.'

For the rest of the afternoon, Piaf spent her time with Claude Figus. Perhaps she wanted to console him, help him 'swallow the pill', to use her term. She even offered, 'In future, Claude, I will write songs for you myself. I know you well. I've figured out what you need.'

Little by little, Claude revealed the traces of a smile once more.

It was that very evening, just as Théo was about to leave, that Piaf suggested he make his home at boulevard Lannes from the next day. As he was there every day anyway, he might as well move his things over. Nello, the chauffeur, would go and pick him up from La Frette and help him to move.

'Would you like that?'

'Yes, O.K.'

The numerous changes taking place at boulevard Lannes triggered a sort of rebirth in the singer. She seemed to be easily made happy, dynamic. She made an effort with her appearance and hair after coming out of hospital. One day, Claude teased her on the subject, 'I'd say you're trying to please a certain someone. Am I wrong?'

Piaf didn't bite. Claude turned to Théo, 'I'll go with you to the station.'

It was on his way; he was heading for Patachou's to perform his songs. En route, Théo asked him what pleasure he got from teasing Edith that way.

'Me? Tease Edith?' Claude expressed surprise.

'Yes, you're implying that she's trying to please someone. It's annoying her.'

'You can't see the lengths she goes to, making herself attractive?'

'Who do you think she's trying to seduce?'

'Who do you think?'

'I don't know.'

'Well, I know!'

Their taxi stopped in front of Saint-Lazare station. Figus stared at my brother, shaking his head, with a knowing smile. Théo began to laugh. 'Come on, tell me. Stop being so mysterious.'

'It's you, Théo. She's trying to please you!'

This revelation left my brother dumbstruck. Edith was going to all this effort to please him? Such a thing seemed completely unreal. Never in a million years would he have imagined a romantic liaison between himself and Piaf. Théo saw himself as a member of the singer's inner circle. For him, their connection was their work. She had decided to 'launch' him after detecting artistic talent in him. And if it were true that she'd been employing all her skills in flirtation, as Figus made him consider, that was just because she felt better in herself, because she had plans and the desire to return to the stage, to find her public once more.

'You've got to be joking, Claude.'

'I've never been more serious.'

'I know she likes me a lot. Otherwise she would never have asked me to move in. I think I'm a distraction for her. But that's a far cry from imagining... You're making it up...'

Figus interrupted, 'I'm not making anything up.'

'She's confided in you?'

'Perhaps...'

Figus revelled in this conversation, in revealing secrets. Finally, he spilled the beans. 'She asked me not to speak to you about it but as you seem so blind, I might as well open your eyes to what's going on. She likes you. And not just as a singer. Just over there. This is where I leave you. I don't want to be late at Patachou's.'

Théo watched the taxi merge into the traffic. The next minute, he was going into the station and heading towards the platforms, walking like an automaton.

Too many things, in too short a time, had changed his existence. He had integrated into the entourage of one of the greatest singers in the world. He was in the process of becoming a singer himself. From the next day, he'd be leaving La Frette in a chauffeur-driven car to move to Paris... And now, completely out of the blue, had come this news: Edith had fallen for him! He would have understood if she'd set her heart on an accomplished entertainer, someone sophisticated, with an exceptional presence, but to fall in love with Théophanis Lamboukas... Of course, Théo was blessed with an attractive physique and a natural elegance, and he was self-assured enough to be guaranteed work and an income, and enough to see himself in an artistic career. However, he still thought himself to be a beginner in the profession, and he couldn't see how Edith Piaf could fall for a singer who was just starting out.

These questions were jostling in his head when he arrived at the house. It was time for our evening meal.

We were at the table. We could tell that Théo had something on his mind. After a while, he told us, 'Edith has invited me to move in with her. I'm moving out tomorrow morning. The chauffeur will come and help me.'

This news fell into a heavy silence. The first conflict had broken out a few weeks earlier, when Théo had announced his decision to become a singer. And now it was all coming to the surface again! When he felt his anger getting the better of him, Papa would begin to breathe heavily, and that's exactly what was happening now I could hear his breathing I could see him staring fixedly at his plate.

'You're going to live with Edith Piaf?'

'Yes.'

'No! No! It won't do!' Papa exploded.

My father and mother dreaded the thought that their son was destroying his life. It had been hard for them to accept him abandoning hairdressing and the security of a 'good job.' They thought he'd taken one more step in the wrong direction, towards a life full of danger! Inevitably, the same debate broke out again around the table. Théo asserted his right to decide for himself what purpose he should give his life. He had given up on his dreams once before when he agreed to enrol at hairdressing school despite the fact that his nature and intelligence were pushing him towards literary studies. In despair at seeing his son slide down a 'slippery slope', Papa had a go at the arty community. In our house, family quarrels never led to threats or insults, but a wall was erected, separating my father and my brother. Without question, we were all miserable now. However, it was Papa who ended it by laying down his arms.

'After all, if it's what you want.'

That evening, I sensed that Théo and I shared this trait in our characters, that although we loved our parents, we would rather face up to them than give in before their demands on *our* life choices. All the more so as we were certain of one thing: no disagreement, no conflict could take away the love which united us, each to the other, and which protected us.

While we were waiting for Théo to make his way on the path he'd chosen, each of us had to cope with this test imposed on us. And if the test was so difficult, it was because Piaf was the only one to know what the path really involved. One day, Théo would be famous and our parents would declare how proud of their son they were. But that evening, in the dining-room at La Frette, fame seemed a long way away, the atmosphere was heavy and the future uncertain.

As for Théo, he had not told us everything. Obviously. He'd only spoken to us about moving house, keeping to himself the secret Figus had revealed that only he could deal with, alone.

7

The next day, as planned, Théo turned up at boulevard Lannes in the chauffeur's car. He had taken his suitcase with him. At once, Edith wanted to show him the wardrobe where he could keep his things. As he was starting to put shirts on hangers, she said to him, 'Leave it. I'll do that.'

She started to fold his pullovers. She took his trousers from the suitcase to make sure the crease was right for hanging.

'I know exactly how shirts should be folded,' she said.

She complimented him non-stop on the choice and quality of his clothes.

If she behaved this way on his arrival, it was to seduce him. Clearly, she figured that a woman should lavish attention on the man she loved if she wanted to please him. One day, Edith expressed this opinion to me, 'Make him a coffee, put sugar in it and stir it in yourself with a little spoon. Fold his things for him. He has to know how much he counts for you.' That's exactly what she was putting into practice with Théo.

Busying herself between the suitcase and the wardrobe, she would pause to give him significant looks from her baby-blue eyes and to sweet-talk him.

'I love that black pullover.'

Obviously, she had no idea that Claude Figus had come clean. And she must have wondered why Théo was acting a little strange. At one point, she asked him, 'Is something wrong? It's as if you've swallowed an umbrella!'

They both fell about laughing, which lightened the atmosphere. Then Edith returned to the fray, trying to get the message across. 'We have the same tastes. We were meant to find each other. Don't you think?'

The scene was very intimate and, thunderstruck, Théo realised how much Piaf fascinated him, not only as a singer but quite simply as a woman. She had an aura, a personality which he had sought in vain among his conquests of an evening at Saint-Germain-des-Prés. As the situation lent itself to confidences, he suddenly opened up about his past whole evenings flitting from one club to the next, passing encounters, one-night-stands. In his defence, he made clear to Edith that his behaviour had sprung from the Algerian war, which had stolen his youth. On his return to Paris, he had felt a strong urge to make up for time lost, to run wild, to take double helpings of life, like a man who's known hunger for too long.

'Then there's the friends you see disappear. Over there, you have the impression that life is nothing, that it hangs by a thread. Which led to the meaningless affairs. I just wanted to make the most of everything, after all that I'd missed out on.'

Then, after letting the silence hang, Edith said, 'Looks like I'm here at the right time.'

She was only half joking. Théo realised that Figus hadn't been telling lies the night before in the taxi.

Edith continued, 'You know, it was the same for me. I had a rough period. And I too was lucky enough to find someone who came into my life at the right moment.'

She was referring to Raymond Asso, the man who had taught her to sing, to improve her diction, to present herself on stage. The man who had launched Piaf, in fact, and who was famous for lyrics such as *Mon légionnaire* or *Le Petit Coquelicot*, sung by Mouloudji.

'He got me back in the saddle,' Piaf remembered sadly. Her eyes brimmed with tears from the memories.

'And then first of all, there was Louis Leplée. The owner of Gerny's Cabaret on rue Pierre-Charron. He literally rescued me from the gutter when I was still just a kid. He was the one who thought up my stage name. 'The Little Sparrow' that was his idea. He made me work hard. He was killed by a bullet from a revolver in his own home. What a tragedy. They even suspected me of being involved! In any case, after Leplée's death, I had nothing any more. I hit rock bottom. Then I had the bright idea of calling Raymond. He turned up instantly. Ah! You could say Raymond was willing to fight on my behalf. He laid siege to music-hall directors to get them to hire me. I was young, lost. If he hadn't been there, to get me out of the mire, God knows where I'd have ended up.'

Edith left a long silence to linger before she felt carried away again by the need to talk.

'Sometimes, you are suffering, you feel you're going nowhere. Then someone turns up and everything works out... At other times, no-one comes. It reminds me of my concert at Olympia. The public gave me an incredible welcome. But when I came back here, I was alone. So I said to myself: what use is all of that? I was still caught up in that incredible emotion; the lights, the applause, the cries of joy, the love you've seen shining in people's faces, that crowd of people. And all of a sudden, I found myself in my huge apartment, not a single person with whom I could share what I had just been through. Enough to make you shoot yourself! Of course, I could have organised drinks back here after Olympia. I could easily have gathered thirty or forty people round me. But having forty people didn't interest me. What I wanted was *one* person. Just one. A man with to share the perfect end to an extraordinary evening. I can't bear solitude, you know that. The gulf is too big between the thousands of people calling your name and the immense void which falls on you afterwards.'

Théo listened to these confidences without saying anything. In his heart of hearts, a voice wanted to call out, 'I am here now! And as long as I am here, you will never be alone!' But he said nothing.

In that 1962 spring, it was decided that Théo would give his numbers a whirl at Patachou's. This meant that Edith came to take up a place in the audience. Of course, she thought of Théo as her protégé but you could also feel that she was motivated by the desire to support him, to see him surpass himself, to fulfil himself, to find himself, so much so that the spectacle was in the auditorium as much as on the stage.

It was the grand spectacle of passion itself.

8

My parents had no idea of what was going on between Piaf and Théo. At home, no-one suspected a thing. We visualised boulevard Lannes as a place frequented by a multitude of theatrical types and variety show entertainers. That's what my brother himself said and, to us, he was just one more newcomer in the singer's entourage.

One Sunday afternoon, we were surprised to see Théo turn up at La Frette on an impulse. He seemed content and slightly nervous at the same time. We all hugged each other, then Théo said, I want to present Edith to you.'

'That would be fine,' replied Papa. 'When did you have in mind?'

'Now.'

We were dumbfounded.

'She's here,' continued Théo. 'Just up the street.'

We followed him to the door into the garden. A white Mercedes came forward to the level of our house. Nello, Piaf's chauffeur, was at the wheel. Beside him was Claude Figus, whom I would get to know later. The chauffeur opened his door and got the car. He then opened the back passenger door. Edith Piaf shifted across until she was on the edge of the seat. She greeted us through the open door with a gesture, staying in the car. My sister and I hung back a little but missed nothing, obviously. Théo took charge of the introductions.

'I would like to present my parents.'

I saw that Piaf blushed she seemed incredibly shy.

'We are pleased to meet you,' said Papa.

'Me too. I have so wanted to get to know you.' Her eyes shone, she was superb.

'We are full of admiration for your talent,' Maman added.

'Thank you.'

From the car, Edith could see Papa's roses peeping over the garden fence. We had so many that La Frette locals called our house the 'Maison des Roses'. It was important to Papa to bless our childhood with a magnificent garden. For him, each season produced its flowers tulips in spring, dahlias in summer. But his favourite was always the queen of flowers, the rose.

In a split second, Papa dived into the garden. He re-emerged with a huge bouquet of roses in his arms, for Edith.

Piaf seemed very moved by the gesture.

'My husband takes care of the flowers,' my mother said.

Théo was touched too, and his deep appreciation for our parents showed in his face. Then he said softly, 'Edith has to go. Me too.'

Papa thanked Piaf. He acted as our spokesman telling her how happy we all were to meet her.

'It was important for me too,' said Edith.

Théo took up a place beside Edith, in the back of the white Mercedes, which nosed up the street again, and he then he disappeared. I remember wondering at that moment why it was my brother who had the honour of sitting in the car beside her. Was the singer trying to make a statement about his importance? Was Théo really just 'one more person in her entourage'?

Théo came back to La Frette the next day he was so impatient to hear our impressions. We told him what had surprised us most: Piaf had seemed to be extremely reserved, almost shy. You would have thought we were dealing with a little girl! Yet the image we'd formed of her beforehand was that of a superstar, blessed with a strong presence, a powerful and contagious energy.

My brother responded that Edith had liked our family very much. So Maman suggested, 'Tell her we've invited her for afternoon tea.'

Apparently the singer loved the idea because shortly afterwards a date was fixed for the following week.

It was a lovely afternoon in June. All the roses were in bloom and the cherry-tree was laden with fruit. Théo and Edith arrived at three o'clock. Papa and Maman had decided to serve tea in the garden and we settled down under the shade of the lime trees.

We all felt intimidated, no-one knew what to say and the silence threatened to last. Maman decided to break the ice. 'When we go to Normandy, my husband likes us to stop at a café with a juke-box. Every time, we play *Je ne regrette rien*.'

It was clear that Edith appreciated my mother's attempt to be nice and that she too was trying her best to get on with my parents. She looked at the garden full of flowers, the cute house, our united family – she who had known so much suffering in her own life. Théo suggested to her that they pick some cherries. 'I know how much you love them.'

Edith followed Théo to the cherry-tree. They ate all the cherries they were able to reach.Edith called Maman, who joined them at the foot of the tree. Maman picked pairs of cherries and hung them on Edith's ears, like children do.

The afternoon finished in merriment and laughter. Théo and Edith then got back into the white Mercedes, where Nello was waiting at the wheel. When he said goodbye, Théo announced that he would accompany Edith back to boulevard Lannes and then he would be sleeping 'at a friend's'. Why did he use this term? No doubt to reassure my parents, in case they were asking themselves what was going on. He had always held them in great respect and, despite the disagreements that had pitted him against Papa, he would do his utmost to avoid upsetting them.

Personally, I was mulling over the recent sequence of events in my brother's life. In a sense, they mirrored my own aspirations. I too wanted to live my own life, how I chose. I was twenty and I had no intention of making a career in Papa's hairdressing salon! I had even got it into my head to embark on the cruise ship *France* as an on-board hairdresser! It was true that the sea frightened me a little but at least this option was on my doorstep. Obviously, my parents were none too happy at the idea. In reality, I was like a fledgling ready to fly from the nest. In the light of Théo's experiences, I was considering my own situation. How do you leave your family without hurting people's feelings? How can you be free without causing pain to those who have protected you for so long?

A week later, Théo let me know that Edith had invited me to come and visit her at home. When it was time to take the train, then a taxi, to be sure of reaching boulevard Lannes on time, I felt more intimidated than ever. Piaf, the renowned Piaf, had thought about me!

At the apartment door, I was welcomed by the man who had been sitting beside the chauffeur during Edith's first visit to La Frette. He was Claude Figus, Théo's friend, someone close to the singer. He treated me like an old friend, using the familiar 'tu' form of 'you'. In fact, seeing how tense I was, he tried hard to put me at ease. But I could see at once how fired up he was with admiration for Piaf and that just made me more nervous!

'I'll go and tell her you're here. Don't worry, she really likes you. She wouldn't have invited you, otherwise.'

A few moments later, I heard voices approaching the lounge where Claude had entered before me. Edith appeared wearing a housecoat of blue velour, a long, comfortable garment with a zip fastener at the front. She greeted me and asked me to sit down next to her on the divan.

'You have a wonderful brother, Christie. And a lovely family.'

As I was shy, she went overboard in kindness. But I didn't feel reassured until the moment Théo joined us in the lounge. Then Suzanne, the cook, announced that Madame's meal was ready. The table was laid in the dining-room. Edith wanted Théo on her right and me on her left. Thanks to her efforts, conversation was lively throughout the meal. As far as I was concerned, I would only speak when asked a direct question. But, in the end, what impressed me most was to see the extent to which Piaf was natural and modest as a person, someone who never put on grand airs, even though she really was someone very special, whose presence lit up a room.

The following Sunday, Piaf invited the whole family to her place. This time, Claude Figus wasn't there. It was just her and us. Edith sat between Papa and Maman, and I had the very clear impression that she wanted to be adopted by the Lamboukas family. Besides, she was so pleasant, so attentive, that all we wanted was to be friends with her. Maman suggested she visit La Frette as often as she wanted so she could benefit from our garden.

We could see the great affection she felt for Théo. But the age difference between them was so big that the possibility of a romance never entered our heads. At the same time, we couldn't help but wonder what this was all about. Edith seemed genuine in wanting to create strong ties with our family. Perhaps, in her eyes, we represented the united family of her dreams. Perhaps she really was an exceptional human being. In our hearts, we felt a bit like we were taking part in something that was beyond our understanding. And as Théo appeared to be happy in his new existence, which consisted of concert plans, rehearsals, relentless work, we only had one desire to do everything possible to support him.

9

Edith took Théo in hand. When she found out he had a tendency to put on weight, she put him on a diet. He didn't complain willingly going for a run on the paths in the Bois de Boulogne. She also made him her student. She gave so much of herself to teach him all she knew of the profession, and above all to transmit that sense of self-discipline that was so important to her. Théo was ready to go on tour. Not only had he made considerable progress at boulevard Lannes by working on his voice and gestures, but he'd also gained experience of an audience since he'd been treading the boards each evening at Patachou's.

Piaf was very focused when she attended my brother's rehearsals. And, because of that, there was complete trust between them. She told Loulou Barrier, who agreed and who thought highly of Théo, 'There is still work to be done but Théo will be ready for the tour in the summer.'

Their feelings had developed a lot further over the course of the weeks spent together, working hard. They had grown closer. Théo had tenderly christened Edith 'his little squirrel'. In response she gave him a watch engraved with the inscription, 'For Théo, from his little squirrel.' Then Théo, in return, bought Piaf an enormous teddy-bear. They gave each other presents all the time. One day she asked him, 'How do you say "I love you" in Greek?'

'You say *sarapo*.'

The Greek word 'to love' is *agapo* and 'I love you' is really *s'agapo*, which can be pronounced 'sarapo'. From childhood, we'd heard Greek spoken round the house. Between themselves, my parents spoke Greek and when we were at the table, Yaya would always ask us to talk in her language, so she could understand what was being said. Often, we mingled French and Greek; we even ended up creating a sort of 'Frengreek'.

'*Sarapo*,' repeated Edith. 'I like that very much. That's what I'm going to call you. Lamboukas is too difficult, too long. Théo Sarapo has a nice sound. It's easy to remember. And you need a name with several '*a*' sounds in it.

She was happy that the name Théo Sarapo had come to her, as if in parallel with her own renaissance to the extent that, from then on, she was over the moon when people sometimes called her 'Madame Sarapo'.

One evening, Théo called me at La Frette to tell me that he and Edith wanted to invite me to dinner. This honour filled me with joy. They had chosen a classy restaurant in the Bois de Boulogne, near the Dauphine gate. I wasn't used to going to such a chic place, full of women in little black dresses, and waiters who wore white gloves and pulled up a chair for you. I was even less used to dining out with Edith

Piaf! Wherever Edith went, people stopped in their tracks to look at her, and that's exactly what happened on this occasion. There was whispering at all the tables when the diners glanced at our trio, eaten up by curiosity. On some occasions, it even happened that people started clapping when we arrived somewhere! But what was most striking, in general, was the friendliness, tenderness even, that Edith inspired. Also, for the most part, the fans controlled themselves and respected her privacy being content with observing her politely in sideways glances.

I was so overwhelmed by such an extraordinary experience that I barely noticed what was on my plate. Edith repeated her compliments about my family. And Théo seemed very relaxed. In fact, I wasn't particularly surprised at being there with the two of them. I was beginning to see Edith as an extremely straightforward and natural woman, who liked people, and who wanted to get to know better anyone close to Théo.

After dessert, we went out to the garden. There was a patio where we could sit and continue chatting in peace and quiet over a coffee. And that's when my brother told me, 'Christie, we have a big announcement to make.'

I was intrigued. A big announcement? Théo was a close friend with the star Edith Piaf, he rehearsed every day with her, he was perfecting his own concert programme at Patachou's, Edith had come to La Frette to see our parents, and she had welcomed me at her table this evening in one of the most elegant establishments in Paris! All these changes were already considerable and I had trouble imagining what sort of 'big announcement' could top them.

Théo turned towards Edith. He took her hand under the table. And they both turned to me as one, with the self-same look on their faces.

'Edith and I are going to be married,' said Théo

They were scrutinising my face for a reaction with such concentration that I felt ill at ease. I had to make a huge effort to hide my astonishment. I didn't want to hurt them for anything in the world by letting out an exclamation of surprise. They looked so happy! But in my heart there was a nagging doubt: the age difference. Edith was forty-six and Théo twenty-six! To the young girl I then was, the contrast was marked between the reality in front of me and my image of two people in love with each other. More so, because I knew that, in theory, Théo didn't want to get married. At least, that's what he'd led us to believe when he returned from Algeria; he wanted to be free and independent, to make the most of life after the long ordeal in military service. In short, I hadn't envisaged that there could be anything between the two of them other than a friendship based on a professional partnership. Even if I forced myself not to let it show, I was dumbfounded.

It was Edith who broke the silence, asking me softly, 'What do you think, Christie?'

What did I think? A thousand reflections jumped into my head.

After all, Edith was only forty-six. She had stayed young at heart. She preferred the company of young people to that of her peers who, as she said with a sigh, talked non-stop of 'their misery and other diseases'. The past seemed to be a source of sadness to her, along with those who embodied it. Besides, communication between us was so easy, even though we were a generation apart. In essence, Piaf was an exceptional being; it would have been stupid to expect her to behave like a mere mortal. Seeing that they were both hanging on the words that would come from my mouth, I ended up replying, 'If you love each other, that's all that matters. Don't you think?'

They exchanged blissful looks, then Edith once more turned to me. 'What about the age difference? Do you think it likely that your parents will be shocked? What's your father going to say?'

Already, I'd almost completely accepted the news. I was quick to reassure Edith. 'Everything will be fine. Papa really likes you. And age isn't important when two people love each other.'

Nevertheless, things didn't go as smoothly as that. From the next day, the sound of shouting echoed round La Frette, where Théo had announced his wedding plans. Papa was not at all happy with this succession of ordeals his son was putting him through. First, Théo had left a solid job and a good position at Elizabeth Arden to throw himself into a career as a singer. Then there had been the decision to live at Edith Piaf's home in Paris, to frequent with an arty milieu, with no security. And now, this marriage!

'Papa! I love Edith! Not someone else!'

'It's not right!'

Papa was furious. Maman held her tongue – she shared her husband's view but she wouldn't get annoyed with her son, not for anything in the world. Me too, I held my tongue, even though I wanted to take my brother's side emphatically. It's true that Edith had captivated me. But it also seemed to me that she and Théo had taken their decision at the right moment. They couldn't allow themselves to wait until Théo was older because it would probably be too late.

One more time, I watched the wall of incomprehension, which I hated so much, come down between Papa and Théo. As the disagreement was turning into a dialogue of the deaf, my brother walked out, leaving in a very bad mood. Our father carried on shouting after he'd gone and it was Maman, as always, who worked hard to calm things down.

For one second, I did wonder whether Théo would ever set foot in the house again but, on the contrary, he came home every evening of the following week. Each evening, the same argument broke out afresh. I went to sit in the kitchen. Maman prepared dinner. The shouting echoed through the dining-room. You sensed that Papa was seeing the end of all of the hopes he'd placed on his son, perhaps rashly. Papa had projected many of his dreams onto Théo and these were now broken in a completely unexpected way. Frustration led him to despair. He must have realised, in his heart of hearts, that he had lost the game, but he carried on getting angry and Théo dug his heels in, trying to win us over and to preserve the tie that held us all together, each to the other. I was grateful to Théo for his attitude; however heated things became, the love itself was still there, that love upon which our upbringing was founded, as was, indeed, our childhood.

That was when there was a new invitation from Edith. The following Sunday, all the family would be welcome to come for lunch at boulevard Lannes.

When the time came to go, I asked Maman, 'What about Papa? Has he changed his mind?'

'No. But I asked him to keep his cool, not to pass comment.'

'That's likely to be difficult.'

'I asked him to be careful if he doesn't want us to lose our son.'

'Théo loves you both, Maman.'

He also loved Edith; Edith, the incarnation of his new life.

As it turned out, I could see Papa's efforts to master his feelings when we arrived at boulevard Lannes. He said nothing. His breathing was rapid. The moment he pointed his finger at the doorbell, I heard Maman whisper in his ear one last piece of advice. 'Please don't spoil the invitation.'

Edith looked her best. She wore make-up and Théo himself had done her hair. She had chosen a skirt and top in teal, a sign that she had gone to some effort as she usually wore black. She was geared up to be friendly and thoughtful.

Lunch passed without incident. It was true that the burning topic had not been mentioned; conversation had turned on all sorts of subjects of little importance, in a pleasant atmosphere, throughout. I understood that this occasion marked the beginning of a new phase, during which my parents, little by little, came to accept their son's marriage plans.

So it was that, when they weren't working, Théo and Edith often came to visit us at La Frette. I had the impression that, far from distancing Théo from his family, Edith was, on the contrary, bringing him closer. She was discovering our little world, she appreciated the sort of people we were, and this attitude allowed Théo to see his own family with fresh eyes. Family was important to Edith. My parents, who had understood this, were now leaning towards acceptance of her as their future daughter-in-law, with all of the generosity of which they were capable.

Then Edith gave us another invitation. Not to boulevard Lannes but to Normandy this time, to a house that had belonged to her until recently and which she had just sold on to Loulou Barrier, her manager. She'd then asked Barrier to let her use the property. 'Can I have it for a weekend, Loulou? I would like to talk to Théo's father. It's the ideal place.'

'No problem, Edith.'

The chauffeur, Nello, came in his white Mercedes to fetch us from La Frette. Edith and Théo were already in Normandy. The house was situated not far from Rouen. The singer was fond of the area, where she had passed some of her childhood. And this property was in the regional tradition. It was a rural property, with a vegetable patch and flower beds. The interior was well appointed. The fireplace created a cosy and comfortable atmosphere. A grand staircase led up to the bedrooms.

When we arrived, the table was already laid. Suzanne and her daughter had come from Paris to prepare a roast and her speciality dish: cheese soufflé. A flan was to follow for dessert.

At Edith's, meals were always generous. Perhaps there was some compensation for those periods of deprivation which would always linger for the singer as a bad memory. Her very temperament pushed her towards eating gourmet food. She loved steak, braised rabbit in mustard sauce, and the classic Northern recipe 'anguille au vert', eel with spinach and herbs. All the same, since that lunch in the countryside, we'd noticed that she ate like a little bird. That's because her doctors had imposed a draconian regime; moreover, each time she gave in to her little weaknesses, she was ill.

The meal was nearly over when she announced, 'I'm going for a little turn around the garden with Papa.'

My father stood up and Edith gave him her arm. They headed peacefully towards the vegetable garden. I watched them from a distance. What were they going to say to each other? I looked at Maman. We had just understood that this invitation to Normandy was a strategy in the campaign and that Edith intended to talk about the wedding with Papa. Later, I learned what was said in the shade of the fruit trees that afternoon.

'Monsieur Lamboukas, I know that you are a very close family and that you are worried about Théo's future.'

Papa could only assent.

'I also know,' continued Edith, 'that he has a strong personality, a good voice, talent. In other words, he has all the qualities it takes to be a great entertainer. That means I can launch his career. Do you think he's the first one?'

She threw Papa a conniving smile. 'I've already launched Montand, Aznavour. And others.'

'I know, I know.'

'When someone has the talent, I can see it straight away. And I have never been wrong. Théo can become a singer. He could even be a film star. In any case, I will take care of him.'

After some thought, Papa replied, 'I'm sure you're right. You have so much experience. You know what you're talking about. And it's true, Théo always loved the music-hall, even as a child.'

'There is something else, Monsieur Lamboukas. Théo and I, we *are* going to get married. He loves me, I love him, it's as simple as that.'

Papa was under her spell; his objections were falling away. He said softly, 'I want you to be happy.'

They came back to the house, arm-in-arm. Their laughter reached us first. They were talking of other things now and clearly as thick as thieves. I exchanged looks with Théo, then with Maman.

We knew it Edith had succeeded in sorting everything out.

10

It was in the town of Reims that the first concert of the summer tour, as envisaged and organised by Piaf, would take place, with Théo and Claude performing in the first half. My parents were really keen to attend the event; they wanted to be in the audience when Théo came on stage. My sister and I went with them. We all set off together for Reims. Unfortunately, our car broke down: the engine started smoking and when he opened the bonnet, Papa burnt his face while unscrewing the radiator cap. As a result, his skin was all red. After the concert, when we all met up at the restaurant, Edith teased him, 'You're looking healthy, Monsieur Lamboukas!'

Without us, Edith, her singers and her musicians continued on a tour that served to pave the way for Olympia in the autumn. Olympia was at that time one of the biggest music-hall venues in Europe. Her director, Bruno Coquatrix, had faced some problems, but it was important to him that Edith was performing, to help her get back on her feet. All the more so because the tour was an enormous success; it was even on its way to being a national event after

Edith had been through Cannes. The papers and magazines were covered with photos of the singer. She was often on Théo's arm and their story intrigued the whole of France. The general public was asking itself the same questions we'd already put to ourselves when we saw the strange couple made by Théo and Edith. But, just like us, people concluded that love ruled and was the only judge needed.

At the end of each spectacle, a difficult ordeal awaited Edith: the fans who crowded round the theatre exit to cheer her and ask for autographs. Théo did his best to protect her, but the path to the car was long, even dangerous. The crowd's movements could be rough, as Edith knew better than anyone. It was even more taxing as she was exhausted at the end of a concert. She only had one desire: to get into the car. However, even sitting in the Mercedes, it wasn't over. A woman glued her face to the window and knocked on the passenger door, screaming, 'Edith! Edith!'

The singer, bone-weary, terrified, murmured, 'Where is Théo?'

'He's signing autographs,' someone said.

'He's got to come now. There's too many people. I need to get back to the hotel.'

She loved her public but the mob frightened her, because its reactions were so unpredictable. Nello, the chauffeur, tried carefully, to start the car. Sometimes, people even tried to lift up the Mercedes!

'What about Théo?' panicked Edith. 'How will he manage to get in?'

Suddenly, in the shadows, she could see a young man making his way with great difficulty, crowded by his admirers. It was Théo. She saw him signing yet another two or three photos. The passenger door was opened for him. At last he could take refuge in the car. Edith let out a sigh of relief and said to Nello, 'Step on it, let's go!'

This tour's success resounded as far as La Frette, where we received a visit from two journalists attached to France-Dimanche. It was in the middle of the afternoon. They arrived with bottles of champagne. They said they wanted to produce a feature article to celebrate the success of Théo and Edith. They built a pyramid of glasses and poured champagne into the topmost one. A champagne fountain! The reporters covered every angle. Maman thanked them and they left.

However the next day at the place de la Gare, there was a bill posted on the news kiosk. It showed Papa and Maman drinking champagne. A headline in large text announced, 'The parents of Théo Sarapo celebrate the imminent wedding of their son and Edith Piaf.'

My father was furious. 'How dare they print such lies!' he shouted, brandishing the magazine.

The telephone didn't stop ringing. A pack of reporters descended on La Frette, sought out our house, and came to the garden door asking for permission to take photos and record interviews for television or radio.

'Monsieur Lamboukas, what do you think about this wedding?'

'I think my son is old enough to know what he's doing!'

'Doesn't the age difference bother you?'

'They love each other. My wife and I wish them all the happiness in the world.'

Everyone in La Frette had an opinion about the event. The hairdresser's son was going to marry Edith Piaf! Some approved, others criticised. There were even people who used the term 'gigolo', which was not pleasant for my brother and was very far from the truth. These conversations – and sometimes bitchy comments, which Maman really hated – came flowing into our hairdressing salon like rivers of words, sometimes sensible, sometimes absurd. Our life was turned upside down by it all. Without having wished it, we found ourselves at the heart of a story that travelled right round the world.

Indeed, the news took over the front pages of all the papers not only in France, but abroad too. Edith was an international star. In that summer of 1962, her face and that of her 'young Greek fiancé' could be seen in the shop window of every newsagent. More than ever, Edith was an icon, whose fate fascinated the public: her deprived childhood; the miracle which had brought back her eyesight; her first steps as a singer; her extraordinary voice; the succession of men on her arm; her health problems; and now these plans to marry a singer twenty years younger than her!

Piaf's health was a serious issue and wasn't getting any better, especially in the context of the tour. Edith had liver disease and also a permanent weakness for gourmet food. As soon as she felt better, the urge to celebrate came over her. The singer would decide to take her friends to a restaurant. Once there, the temptation was great to order the dishes her doctors had banned. At first, she let Théo choose what she would eat. But she would always end up ordering the famous braised rabbit in mustard sauce that she so wanted the rest of the world to discover. Inevitably, the next day, she would fall into a hepatic coma. And Théo would have to take her to hospital as an emergency. In general, she managed to get back on her feet quite quickly. She would ask for her musicians at her bedside... All the other patients had to do was to enjoy the rehearsals, the party atmosphere that suddenly ruled the ward. Edith had the gift of imparting strength and courage into the hearts of those who were lucky enough to hear her.

Autumn 1962 was to be marked for her by a national event, the Grand Gala at the Eiffel Tower, organised for the premiere of the film *The Longest Day*. Several directors had combined efforts to shoot this huge international production to honour the glory of the allied landings in Normandy, at a time when memories of the war and the liberation were once more in everyone's thoughts. Not only thoughts, in fact; the Normandy beaches were still too wrecked by battles to be used as film sets, and so the scenes of the landings were actually shot in Corsica. The principal roles were played by a host of world-famous actors, such as Richard Burton, John Wayne, Robert Mitchum and Mel Ferrer. Even Sean Connery showed up, before he became known for the James Bond series. France was represented by Arletty, Jean-Louis Barrault or maybe Bourvil. The film premiere was to be heralded with a big party, whose object was not only publicity but patriotism. One of the organisers turned up at boulevard Lannes saying that Piaf definitely had to sing on that evening.

'Where?' asked Edith.

'At the top of the Eiffel Tower.'

Edith hesitated. She was exhausted. At the same time, she was aware of what was at stake in such a public tribute to the glory of the Allies. She turned to Théo. 'Would you like that?'

'If you're not too tired.'

He thought the idea was fantastic, he was keen. But if he had felt that Edith had no strength left, he would have advised against her taking on this challenge. He would even have stopped her. As it happened, he had the impression that she was up to it.

'Then let's do it.'

The organiser was on cloud nine.

Edith prepared as if she was going on tour again, doubling the number of rehearsals. On the day itself, enormous crowds spread throughout the whole of Paris. The Champ de Mars was swarming with people. Each quarter was equipped with loudspeakers adjusted for maximum volume. I happened to be at the Trocadéro with friends. The atmosphere was incredibly noisy and exhilarating. Suddenly, a presenter announced that Piaf was going to sing *Non, je ne regrette rien* and a stillness fell on the city a striking contrast. After a few seconds of absolute silence, Edith's voice was set free from the speakers. The magic worked instantly. An audience of millions listened, as if transported. Parisians from all walks of life stopped whatever they were doing to find comfort in the melody that everyone knew, in the words that bore witness to a sentiment each of us could relate to, finding an echo, no doubt, in our own lives.

At the end of the song, a huge clamour rose across the whole of Paris.

11

Piaf was happy to be back on stage again after a full year of ill health. During her summer tour, the public had thought her more and more fragile, but at the same time determined to enjoy the happiness that life offered her. They made sure they kept her company, encouraged her, applauded her ever more enthusiastically. Then the couple returned to Paris, where rehearsals started again at boulevard Lannes, this time with the concerts at Olympia in mind.

Edith realised that launching a singer represented a great risk. If it didn't work out, a career was ruined, perhaps even a life. In Théo's case, this risk was increased by the fact that he was new to the profession. After all, he was still curling hair for Elizabeth Arden at the beginning of the year. He'd had to learn everything in just a few months, although under Edith's protection, it's true, and she'd played the rôle of Pygmalion with great enthusiasm. But the professionals thought the metamorphosis to be complete: Théo had become a talented singer. There was, however, an important test to pass, that of the consecration.

As for Olympia, that was rather different from a tour in this legendary theatre, an entertainer was judged by all of Paris, an audience without pity which was a considerable challenge. It was all very well for Théo to sing at Patachou in the springtime, and then in numerous villages throughout France but Paris was a different kettle of fish. Hence the extra rehearsals in the afternoon that Edith imposed on him and which sometimes drained him of all his strength.

She was the one who had chosen the outfit in which he would appear black shirt and black trousers. 'Black is expressive,' she said.

Since then, this combination was always associated with my brother's stage persona. This is what he wore in the autumn of 1962 on the huge posters pasted all along the Champs-Élysées, in the different quarters of Paris, and as far away the suburbs. He was also in photographs in Edith's company, him so tall and her so petite. It was their spectacle, their Olympia, and the event was associated with their love for each other. The evening began with some classic music-hall acts of the time magicians, contortionists. Then Théo would wrap up the first half as a guest artist – Claude Figus had in turn disappeared from the programme. I should explain what being guest artist at Olympia meant at that time! It was an activity reserved, in theory, for established artists. But Théo was confident; Edith supported him with all her heart.

The day before the premiere, she said to him, 'We don't sing the day before a concert.'

They decided to allow themselves a day off going for a peaceful walk in the Bois de Boulogne. In the afternoon, Théo agreed to give several interviews. And then the evening was spent just the two of them.

The next day, they were both calm and relaxed, despite the waves of excitement rising up around them. They reached Olympia together with time to spare. They wanted to check that everything was in order, and also to get to the concert hall without having to get past the crowd. Edith had received innumerable telegrams wishing her luck, signed sometimes by unknowns and sometimes by great stars from the worlds of arts and variety. She knew that artistic Paris would be present in the audience, but she had asked that no-one mention to Théo the famous names who'd be there, for fear that he'd lose his concentration and go to pieces at the thought of singing in front of such a galaxy of stars.

For the last few minutes before he was called to the stage, my brother was very nervous. To try and calm himself, he slipped out of the corridors and trod the boards behind the curtain. During this time, the audience arrived. The hubbub filled the auditorium. At one point, eaten up by curiosity, Théo opened the curtain to see who was there. The first people he caught sight of were the couple Yves Montand and Simone Signoret. Théo closed the curtain again quickly. He didn't want to know who else had turned up. He went back to the corridors and said to Edith, 'You know who I've just seen?'

'Yes.'

'You never told me!'

'I didn't tell you because I knew it would make you nervous. And for me, the only person who counts is you.'

Théo took Edith in his arms. They kissed each other.

'For me too, the only one who counts is you.'

Edith looked up at him. 'This evening you're going to sing for me and only for me. And you'll see, that's how you'll win them over.'

I was in the hall with Papa, Maman and my sister. Eyes riveted on the red curtain, we held our breath. The first acts of the evening were performed. Then the curtain opened abruptly and Théo appeared in the spotlight, stunning in the dark stage costume Edith had suggested. The audience gave him a polite reception. A second later, my brother launched into his numbers, giving his all. His last song was greeted with thunderous applause, bursting out from all four corners of the auditorium. Papa couldn't hide his emotions any longer, and the eyes of Maman and I filled up with tears. The gamble had paid off: Théo's metamorphosis was complete.

I found out later that Edith was waiting for Théo with a glass of water at the end of his act. But Théo wanted to take Edith in his arms at once and only someone's quick reactions saved the glass of water in mid-air. In the hall, the applause continued.

'They want you back on,' murmured Edith. 'Go on! They're yours…'

The curtain re-opened several times on Théo Sarapo, who smiled for the audience, holding out his arms wide. The public shouted, 'Théo! Théo!' I felt happy, relieved. Maman and Papa too.

After the intermission, the lights dipped and silence fell in the theatre. When Edith materialised in the spotlight, frail and vulnerable in her little black dress, but obviously happy, the entire audience stood as one and the applause broke out. The standing ovation lasted half an hour! Edith thanked them all politely. You could see how important it was for her to be there once more. When the shouts of 'Bravo!' had died down, she started her recital. Her voice, her songs touched people in their deepest core. But she was also crowned with the glory of her own legend, the happy and sad events that had studded her life, while her vulnerability, more visible than ever, gave an air of 'swansong' to the spectacle, a heart-wringing quality in perfect harmony with her dramatic personality.

That evening there were encores without end. The concert played to a full house for weeks. The word in Paris was that some people bought seats for repeat performances. Like the summer tour, Olympia was a triumph and the couple formed by Edith and Théo Sarapo existed on stage from that moment on, just as much as in life.

As far as I was concerned, I admired Edith more and more, seeing her as a truly courageous woman, capable of surpassing herself. Knowing from Théo how weak she was physically, I was impressed by the power she exuded on stage, in the incredible love affair linking her with her public. This mix of energy and vulnerability was what best characterised Edith. In fact, underneath her frailty, she was blessed with great vitality and it was this strength, this appetite, which had the power to destroy her.

Shortly afterwards, when the spectacle at Olympia was in full swing and playing to a full house every evening, I found myself one afternoon at boulevard Lannes in the company of Edith, Théo and Loulou Barrier. Michel Emer arrived. Michel was a well-known singer-songwriter, in Edith's circle since before the war and already the composer of many of her songs. He seemed carried away with enthusiasm. He went straight to the piano and sat down, saying, 'I have a song for you!'

He meant, 'For Edith and Théo.' He was already putting a sheet of paper on the music-stand. His fingers ran across the keyboard and he began to sing.

We listened to the whole song. It was absolutely perfect – at least in my opinion – even if I kept that to myself for the time being. Michel was right: the song told the truth about their life together. I could see that Théo and Edith were also excited. Loulou Barrier too.

Edith said straight away, 'Stay at the piano, Michel. We'll give it a whirl right now.'

Without further ado, they began to sing:

À quoi ça sert l'amour ?
On raconte toujours
Des histoires insensées
À quoi ça sert d'aimer ?

(What is the point of love?
We hear so much these days
Of mad and stupid ways
What is the point of love?)

It was truly a wonderful song, which would soon be on everyone's lips and all our radios. The most extraordinary thing for me was to see its birth, in the emotion of an unexpected discovery. After a few attempts, Edith was so happy that she said, 'We'll put it into our repertoire.'

That was the beginning of a famous number that was to be repeated until the end of the season at Olympia. Edith would stop in the middle of her recital and wait for silence. Then she would turn sweetly to the wings and call, 'Théo.'

Théo would reappear, emotional, elegant, happy. He would come close to her and they would sing as a duo, *A quoi ça sert l'amour?* Edith and Théo would be forced to give encore after encore. The fashion for duets was thus launched in Paris!

12

'I want to get married in your church,' murmured Edith.

She was a believer, Catholic, but her own church would not marry her because she was divorced. In any case, she had adopted our family and our religion suited her perfectly. This was how she came to be on Théo's arm in front of Father Meletios, the Metropolitan head of the Greek Orthodox Church of Paris, on rue Georges-Bizet, the same place where my brother and I had been baptised. It was on the 9th October 1962, during their concert run at Olympia. A civil ceremony was held at the Town Hall in the 16th arrondissement and you only have to click on YouTube these days to see the great occasion once more thanks to the newsreels of the time: the engaged couple getting out of the white Mercedes at the entrance to the Town Hall; their tricky route through a horde of people going wild; the onlookers glued to the railings and talking to the reporters; the overworked police; the close-up shots of my brother's face; and at last, the youthful emotion of the star singer, whose inimitable voice can be heard finally asking the reporters, politely, 'Come on guys, enough, or I won't be able to get married! You've already taken millions of photos!'

I nearly didn't make it to the ceremony because there was such a crush all around the Town Hall. I had come with my sister in the car belonging to the singer Charles Dumont, who had been close to Piaf for years and who'd written many of her songs, including the famous *Non, je ne regrette rien* and *Mon Dieu*. The problem was that when we arrived at avenue Henri-Martin, all of the access routes were blocked. Six police cars had been mobilised in case of possible incidents. Our vehicle was stopped by an officer of the law and Charles pleaded our cause in his most winning tones. 'We are wedding guests, Officer!'

'No-one is allowed through. Make a U-turn and keep driving.'

I leaned towards the doorway. 'But I'm Théo Sarapo's sister! The bridegroom!'

'Yeah, yeah. And I'm his cousin. Get driving or I'll be giving you a caution.'

'Don't you recognise me?' Charles persisted.

The policeman scrutinised him carefully. As well as writing lyrics for stars, Charles was well-known as a singer himself.

The officer nodded his head. 'Yes, I do recognize you. Didn't you write...'

'*Non, je ne regrette rien* – is it a song you like?'

'Who doesn't like it? You can go through.'

After signing the register, which sealed their union, the married couple appeared for a few minutes on the Town Hall balcony and the quarter resounded with a million 'Bravos'. Then the procession headed towards rue Georges-Bizet and the church where Father Meletios was waiting for them, with a moving ceremony that was shown all round the world.

The wedding was followed by a reception at boulevard Lannes. Then, that same evening, Edith and Théo were on stage at Olympia!

Yet, Edith was very tired. She felt that her strength could disappear at any moment. During the tour, she had said to my brother, 'If I hadn't met you, I could never have kept going.'

At this time, the series of concerts was about to end, despite dogged pursuit by Bruno Coquatrix, who would have liked nothing better than to add on more dates after such a triumph. He badgered Edith so much to stay on at Olympia in November that Théo had to put his foot down. 'At the end of October, we stop.'

He was worried about her, he could see how much she needed to rest. Everyone knew she was in bad shape. She was paying for past excesses, the drugs she'd been given in the old days to enable her to keep going when she was on stage, the serious car accident that she'd had with Moustaki four years earlier. She suffered from liver problems, was ill, had frequent intestinal obstructions. Admittedly, she was only forty-six years old, but she had already lived many lives – and many demanding lives, at that.

During the period that followed her wedding, Edith and I became very close. The fact that they'd made their union official consolidated the family connections, and, as I've said before, she liked being in the company of young people. We often went walking in the Bois de Boulogne, just the two of us. I was aware of the extent to which her past haunted her; any ordinary scene could make her traumas resurface. On one such occasion, when we could hear the shouting and laughter of children as we passed near a playground, she tensed up suddenly and said in a shaky voice, 'I can't bear hearing children. Come on, Christie, let's go home.'

They brought back the memory of her two-year old daughter, whom she'd lost when she herself was only nineteen. The toddler had succumbed to meningitis, I think, leaving Edith deeply traumatised. The notion of childhood troubled her and gave birth to mixed emotions, which came out in my presence. My youth seemed to revive her maternal instinct. On the one hand, she couldn't help thinking about her daughter, who would have been older than me if she'd lived; on the other, she wanted to consign this terrible mourning to oblivion.

Time passing tormented her. Once, when I went into the room where the piano held pride of place, I found her in the company of a tall, slim, older man. They were talking in low voices, sitting side by side on the sofa. I was invisible. After the visitor had left, Edith said, 'Do you know who that was?'

'No.'

'Raymond Asso! He launched me. I've known him since before the war.'

'Do you see him often?'

'No. This was a rare event. I'm afraid of being dragged down into old age, you know. I would rather stay among young people and live in the present.'

Living in the present, for her, meant singing. She hoped she could live in the present forever and die on stage because, for her, singing and living were one and the same.

One day, at boulevard Lannes, she took me to one side and murmured in my ear, 'Théo and I want to talk to you.'

I had an inkling of what the subject might be. I knew that my parents had confided their worries in her about my need for freedom and independence. A need which had only become more marked since my brother's marriage. I had not given up my idea of setting sail on the cruise ship *France* as an onboard hairdresser, which worried them even more. And as they trusted Edith, they hadn't thought twice about asking for her advice one Sunday when she and Théo were at La Frette.

A discussion took place between the newly weds and me. In reality, this consisted mostly of Edith talking. 'Your parents have said you want to set sail on the *France*, Christie. Is it true?'

'I'm twenty, Edith! I'm not going to work in Papa's salon all my life. Théo's managed to get out of La Frette all right, hasn't he?'

Théo gave an understanding smile. Edith continued, 'But, the *France* isn't such a good idea, you know. Do you think you can put up with being so far away from everyone you know for weeks at a time?'

It's true that I wasn't completely convinced myself.

'We want to suggest something to you,' said Théo.

'Come and live with us,' Edith followed on. 'Would you like that?' I couldn't believe my ears.

Edith carried on, 'You could have your own room. The one Aznavour used to have, next to the library. You would be independent. You could do what you like, accountable to no-one. And your parents would be reassured if they knew you were near us.'

I was trying to gather my thoughts, after the first shock of the idea.

'Think about it.'

'I've thought about it!'

'You should think about it all the same… And let us know when you've decided.'

This solution suited me perfectly as, to be honest, I wasn't really ready to travel across oceans or to leave my parents behind. All that I wanted was to put a little distance between us, to have the feeling I was in charge of my own life.

A short while after this exchange, I had the pleasure of telling Edith and Théo that I was going to accept their invitation. This made Edith happy. She said to me, 'In any case, you can always give it a try. You'll soon see whether you like it or not.'

At the end of October, I left La Frette with my belongings to take up residence, in my turn, at boulevard Lannes.

Leaving my parents turned out to be much harder than expected. I felt remorse. The first nights at Edith and Théo's, I kept waking up in tears, like a little girl who wanted her Papa and Maman. I had to take myself in hand. 'You're twenty years old, Christie! You'll be an adult soon! You're better off here than on a boat, suffering sea-sickness!' Straight away, Edith reacted very protectively towards me. No doubt she understood that I needed help getting over a difficult hurdle. Besides, she was very family-orientated and keen on the idea of solidarity.

That didn't stop me from being shy. When I first moved into boulevard Lannes, I hardly dared come out of my room! When Théo and Edith called me for dinner, I was frightened of disturbing their privacy. And I was still so much in awe of Edith, despite the trouble she took to set me at ease. 'If you need anything, Christie, just tell me. Or let Théo know O.K.?'

In the afternoon, they stayed in the house to work and Piaf said to me, 'Pull up a chair and listen.'

These were not intensive sessions, because they had no more concerts to give at Olympia. Besides, they were often interrupted by visiting musicians who came to perform their pieces. But there was always something that could be better; Piaf was a perfectionist, she never stopped wanting to improve, to advance. In any case, my main activity at this time was to be there at these rehearsals. I saw the methods Piaf used to make my brother work. For me, the experience was inspiring, and I didn't miss an eye-blink, even if there was nothing in the present to suggest that one day I too would sing and make records.

Edith and Théo were in the habit of passing their evenings peacefully at home. Suzanne, the cook, would prepare a tasty dinner. Sometimes, there would be guests. Then Edith would tell Suzanne, 'Make your roast beef. With little potato rissoles, green beans and Provençal tomatoes.

To provide a dessert, Suzanne would visit the best pastry-maker in the 16th arrondissement.

Guests would almost always be from the entertainment world, and often famous couples. I remember one dinner with Jeanne Moreau and the fashion designer Pierre Cardin, another with Dalida and Lucien Morisse from the television channel Europe 1. These superstars, who admired Edith tremendously, took care to show some modesty in her presence. At table, everyone talked shop and only shop cinema, music, variety. Among the regulars were Sasha Guitry and Jean Cocteau. Loulou Barrier was the one who insisted that Edith invited high society to her home; she and Théo rarely went out to receptions.

In November, when the series of Olympia concerts was over, Théo had the idea of renovating the apartment. He knew that Edith was fed up with the cheap carpets and faded wallpaper. In the time she had lived alone, she'd never plucked up courage to throw herself into the work of re-decorating. It was enough for her then to sing and to have friends around her. But now that she had Théo, she was tired of the same old surroundings and was no longer afraid of upheaval.

It was Théo who took care of everything. We moved to the George V for the duration of the work. In this luxury hotel, I had a beautiful room next to their suite. I still remember the colours of my new setting: blue, cream, gold traces around the windows and doors. We stayed there for a month. Théo had taken a completely fresh look at the decoration of the apartment. He supervised the worksite, day after day.

The rest of the time, the three of us went out together. They took me everywhere. Sometimes, I wondered why they hampered their lives with a 'kid' like me. Yet each time, I realised that Edith wanted to take me under her wing, to give me affection and be loved in return. She had an enormous need to be loved. Her popularity had soared yet again on the occasion of her wedding in the middle of the Olympia run, and it really seemed that the French public was hanging on every event in her life, on her manner of seeking happiness, on the evolution of her state of health. Everyone was talking about her, and about her life with Théo Sarapo. For all that, being worshipped by a public of millions was not enough. In this domain, she was insatiable.

I also think that if she welcomed me this way into her private life, it was for the love of her husband. She thought it good for him to have someone fresh and innocent around, to offer calm between incessant visits and the tensions that filled their lives, which was inevitable in their profession. One day, Edith confessed to me, 'You know, Christie, I don't like women much. And I wouldn't like it much if there was another woman in my home, coming between my husband and me. But you, you're different. I like you. That's why you're here.'

One evening, we had dinner in front of the television. This was unusual, but Edith particularly wanted to watch a programme that was on at dinner-time. Francis Lai was with us. We were having a good time, full of fun and friendship. All of a sudden, smoke rose from behind the television. I rushed to the bathroom, returning with a wet towel

In Théo's arms, Édith felt safe. God wanted to shower them with a sincere, true love at the end of their life.

'Being loved by Théo and singing; you see, Christie, nothing else matters to me. You don't need a lot of men in your life. One is enough.'

Théo rehearses the song 'Pense à moi,' with input from Édith. 'That's good! Open your arms wide, occupy the space, give yourself to the audience!'

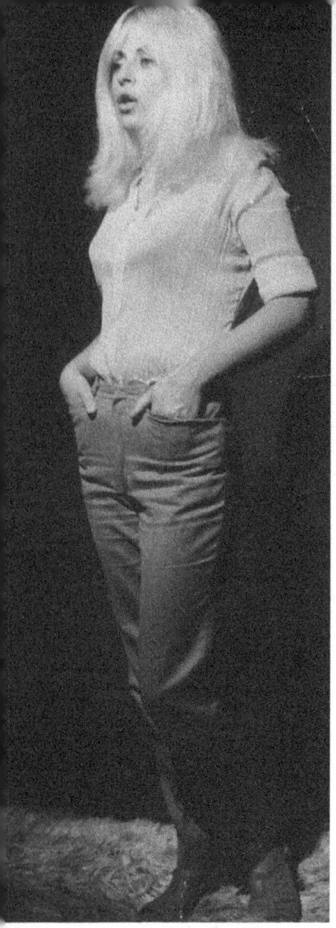

'Sing something for me, Christie.' Édith's simple words encouraged me to write and sing in the grand era of yé-yé. *(d.-r.)*

With Édith and Théo at Mougins; the last good moments spent together. 'I wouldn't like it much if there was another woman in my home, coming between my husband and me. But you, you're different. I like you. That's why you're here.' *(Ph. Paul Guglielmo)*

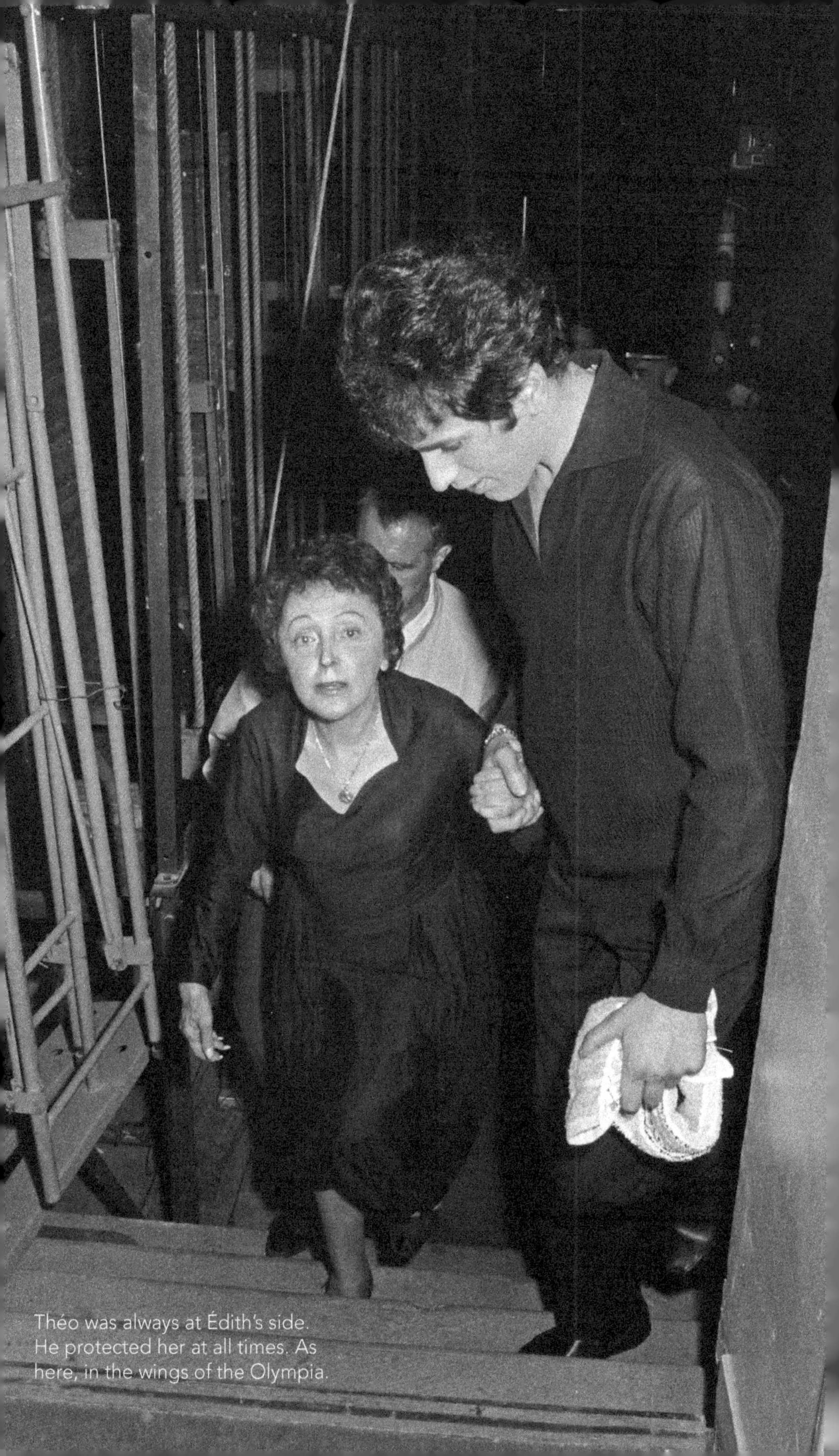

Théo was always at Édith's side. He protected her at all times. As here, in the wings of the Olympia.

Marlene Dietrich was a witness at her wedding to singer Jacques Pills, in 1952, in New York. The two of them confided in each other. 'She was one of the best friends I've ever had,' Édith told me.

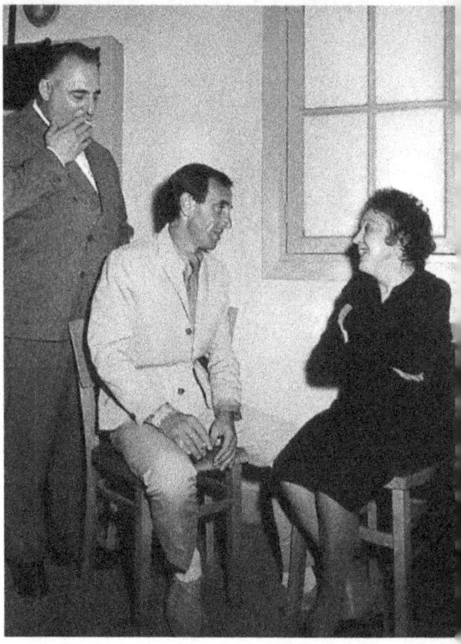

With Bruno Coquatrix and Charles Aznavour in Nice. 'I always believed in him,' she told me. 'It wasn't easy for him at the start, I had to encourage him. 'You'll get there! Look at me, I found it difficult too, in the beginning.'

On tour at Arcachon, arm-in-arm with singer Claude Figus, her secretary, and with Théo, in the company of Francis Lai. Édith murmured to me, 'Francis isn't bad. He's very talented. What do you think? You'd be good together.'
(ph. Photo-Lecture)

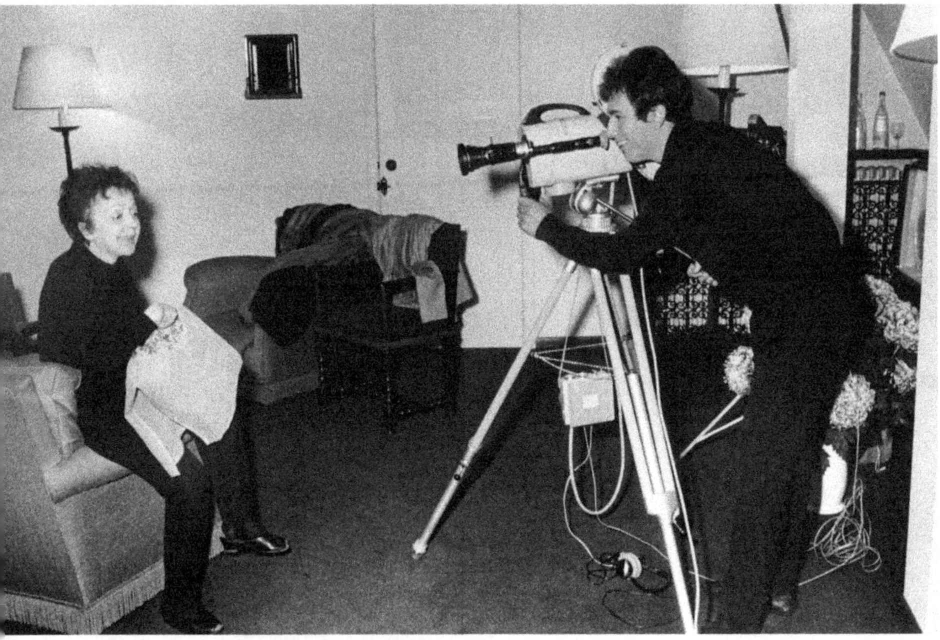

Édith and Théo, two children happy to be together. 'You see, Christie, embroidery de-stresses me and Théo is so contented, filming me with the camera I gave him.'

From 17th to 19th August 1962, Édith was recovering from acute indigestion at the Notre Dame de la Compassion Clinic, Besançon. 'See,' she stated, 'I'm fine. And anyway, I'm with Théo.'

9th October 1962, Édith and Théo said 'I do', according to Greek ritual, in the church in rue Georges-Bizet. That day, Édith became Madame Lamboukas.

Arrival at Nice Airport, 31st May 1963. Théo rented the villa La Serena, at Saint-Jean-Cap-Ferrat so Édith could rest and prepare for her triumphant comeback to the stage. A comeback in which she believed, knowing that Théo would be at her side.

At La Serena, with everyone already there; Francis Lai, Nöel Comaret, Christian, Édith's driver, Christiane, the chambermaid (with her baby), Simone Margantin, the nurse, Suzanne, the cook, Danielle Bonel, the secretary and Marc, her husband. On Théo's lap, Sophie, the miniature poodle he'd given Édith and which I carried on stage when I presented the show.

'À quoi ça sert, l'amour ?' The last performance at Olympia in September 1962. We couldn't stop clapping. 'They're yours,' Édith told Théo.

When she sang, 'La Foule', Édith carried me away with her. Her charisma and emotion made feel involved in the story.

Loulou Barrier, Théo, Charles Dumont, Danielle and Marc Bonel at Père-Lachaise Cemetery, 14th October 1963. 'Mais toi, t'es le dernier, mais toi, t'es le premier! It's you, who are the last one, and it's you, who are the first! You're the one I wanted, you're the one I needed, you're the one I'll always love…'

to wrap round the appliance, which was catching fire. Théo pulled out the plug then, grabbing a bottle of water, used it like a fire extinguisher. By chance, I caught Edith's glance at him, full of admiration for her Prince Charming, the man with whom she was so much in love.

We left the George V hotel to find, on returning to boulevard Lannes, the apartment as new, redecorated according to Théo's tastes – and his tastes were somewhat individual. Doors and windows were repainted white. In the library, hung with red velvet, the antique books that Théo had always loved were lined up on long rows of shelving. This was their favourite room. It contained a stereo hi-fi, red armchairs and black armchairs, a sofa, lights which gave out a beige, relaxing hue, and the television set. Théo had covered the dining-room walls with salmon fabric and the floors with Persian rugs. To furnish it, all three of us went to buy Louis XVI pieces, as well as furniture for a Louis XVI bedroom. Edith liked the table to be set at meal-times with candle-sticks and pretty table linen, embroidered with flowers. The lounge was in beige tones, with a golden fitted carpet, covered by an Oriental rug that warmed up the ambience. It goes without saying that the grand piano was always in its place. As for their bedroom, from then on it was upholstered in grey-blue velvet, with royal blue curtains. Théo also had blue carpets put down in the small adjoining room, a sort of boudoir where Edith took refuge, to find peace, to put on her make-up or to receive her masseur. After this room, came their bathroom, decorated in green marble.

Edith and Théo were delighted with their love-nest. They enjoyed living and working there. They really appreciated being able to relax, to listen to records, read, swap confidences. If Edith Piaf had begun life in the poverty of rue de Belleville, she would end it in fame and comfort, to a great extent thanks to Théo.

13

One night, there was a knock on my bedroom door. The alarm clock showed 5a.m. A little scared, I sat up in my bed. The door opened slowly to a crack of light. The petite silhouette of Edith was outlined in the frame.

'Christie...'

Edith came closer. 'Christie, I can't get to sleep. Would you talk a little with me? I know it's not a good time but...'

She had got up carefully, so as not to wake her husband, and slipped out of her bedroom, coming straight to mine. We headed for the library in silence. She looked at me sweetly. 'It's the first time I've woken someone at five in the morning and received a smile in return.' She also said, 'I'm going to make a cup of tea.' She slipped out, remarking as she went, 'Wrap yourself in a blanket or you'll catch cold.'

I snuggled up under a blanket in one of the armchairs. The atmosphere was warm, intimate. Théo's collection of books was a reminder of his presence. Edith came back from the kitchen with a tray that she placed on the coffee table. She had chosen an oriental teapot and brought two cups. She played mother and poured the tea – Chinese tea that she knew how to prepare to perfection. For me, still so young, for me, a nobody, it was very touching to be served by this woman who was adored by the whole world.

We were face to face, each of us in an armchair, each of us curled up in a blanket; the atmosphere was relaxed as we didn't think anyone would disturb us so early in the morning.

'I left Théo asleep,' said Piaf in a low voice. 'He works so hard. He needs to rest if he wants to take care of his voice.'

Moving on to a different subject, she continued, 'Have you had any news of your boyfriend?'

She was referring to a boy I'd dated without really being in love with him. 'I told him it was over.'

'When?'

'When I came to live here. I wrote him a goodbye letter.'

'Why did you do that?'

'It didn't seem worth carrying on. I felt… lost.'

'I'm sure he'll call you.'

'I don't think so, Edith.'

'You don't think he'll want to see what you are like?'

'We'll see…'

I was troubled. Edith seemed so sure of herself! I knew she had a sixth sense which allowed her to read people's innermost feelings like an open book, but that was a far step from figuring out the intentions of a boy she had never met! Well! She was spot on! One day, to my great surprise, the young man made contact again to see how I was doing. But too much water had passed under the bridge.

After this brief exchange about my love life, Edith let the silence grow. Then she put down her cup and I saw that she felt under pressure. Within minutes, she started to cry softly. She murmured, mopping up the tears, 'It's Théo.'

'What about him?'

'I love him so much. I'm so happy with him. But I'm older than him and the thought torments me. I'm forty-six and he's twenty-seven, you know what I mean?'

She sobbed more loudly. She had been overcome by anxiety earlier on, when she couldn't sleep. That was why she had got up and slipped out of her bedroom to come and knock on my door. She couldn't bear to face this torment on her own. She needed to pour her heart out to someone.

I left my armchair and came very close to her. 'You love each other, Edith. Age doesn't matter.'

'He is so good-looking! He has so much charm. Can you imagine if another woman comes into his life?'

She sighed. She could not shake off these gloomy premonitions, familiar to many women, even stronger in her because the situation was complicated by the age difference, that disparity which commonly provoked the first reaction when thinking about their marriage.

'There are so many young, beautiful women. They will try and steal him from me.'

'Are you thinking of any woman in particular? Have you noticed anything?'

‘You think I don’t see them? How they look at him! You think I don’t realise?’

‘But what about Théo? Does he respond to these looks? Have you seen him take an interest in someone else?’

‘No.’

‘There you are then.’

I did my best to reassure her. Not for one second did I doubt my brother’s faithfulness to his wife. I had every reason to know that Théo was an honest man.

‘You don’t need to worry, Edith. The opposite, in fact. You should make the most of your happiness. You married a young man who prefers living with a mature woman, that’s all there is to it.’

She dried her tears with a little embroidered hankie that she pulled out of her sleeve. ‘Do you think so?’

Piaf, the great Edith Piaf, seemed like a frightened little girl, curled up under the pale beam of the lamp. She needed someone to hold her hand. Happy with Théo, she feared seeing that happiness disappear. She said to me, almost whispering, ‘You don’t need a lot of men in your life. One is enough. One is enough for me.’

Still in a low voice, she carried on opening up her feelings. ‘I have never loved before like I love Théo. Oh! I’ve admired more than one fellow in the past. God knows I’ve been in love. And more than once. But my feelings for Théo are different from anything I’ve felt before. This love is much deeper. In any case, no man has known how to love me the way Théo does. He is so attentive. He is so good that I forget how beautiful he is. He looks after me all the time.

He waits on me hand and foot. He has endless patience.

Her distress was beginning to ease off. Edith was getting her colour back. After consoling her, I went back to my armchair. She carried on, 'Actually, I am lucky. I never imagined this could happen! Of course, I believe in love. That's nothing new. But to have met Théo! This marvellous marriage. It's extraordinary.'

She fixed me with her blue gaze. Her slim arm slipped out of the blanket so she could raise it. 'I want to help him climb higher. While I'm still here. Before anything happens to me. Afterwards, he will fly on his own wings...'

I interrupted her. 'Don't talk like that. You frighten me. You're young too. And your success is enormous.'

Memories were troubling her. 'I'm not young, Christie. You are, you're young. And you grew up in a loving family. Anyone can see that you were protected by your Papa, your Maman, your brother. By your family, so united, so warm, so courageous. I never knew anything like that. You know I was born in the street, don't you? My father had girls everywhere. Wherever he went, there were girls. As for my mother, she was a drug addict. I saw her hitch up her dress to use a needle through her stocking.

This horrible image shocked me especially when described by Edith in her dark, dramatic voice.

'You saw her do that?'

'When I was a little girl. I didn't see that sort of thing later because she left me on my own.'

'Did you love your mother?'

'I wanted to help her. But I was very young when she left. She was a singer. After she left, I was sent to my grandmother in Normandy. My grandmother! She kept a brothel in Bernay. The girls used to look after me. They were nice. They used to buy me treats all the time. They used to sit me on their laps. I don't like people making fun of prostitutes, or sneering at them. That makes me see red. People have no idea what these girls have gone through in their lives to reach such a state. It's so easy to laugh at others when you want for nothing, when you've been lucky enough to see the light of day in a good family.'

I guessed that, in the past, Edith must have suffered herself from being scorned by the sort of people who thought themselves superior just because they were comfortably off.

'Once you've started that way of life, it's hard to get out of it. What saved me was my voice. Without my voice, perhaps I'd have finished up like them.'

Edith Piaf a prostitute... So difficult to imagine such a thing! And yet there must have been some basis for these reflections. Listening to her talk this way, I had the impression I was a privileged person, born into a cosy cradle, cosseted by Papa and Maman – and it was true, actually. She was born on rue Belleville, in a dark quarter, bristling with danger.

I would have liked to relieve her of these melancholy memories. But it was clearly impossible. That was her life. Nothing could be done to change it. All I could do was listen, let her know that she was loved. She continued to murmur confidences, while we both huddled in our armchairs, each in a blanket.

'My grandmother didn't put milk in my feeding-bottles but a mixture of water and wine. She said that would kill the germs. And all of a sudden, I went blind. I couldn't see anything. I was nine years old.'

'You were given treatment?'

'I had a form of keratitis. An inflammation of the cornea. The doctor couldn't do much. Every Sunday, my grandmother and her girls said prayers on my behalf. After a year, they took me on a pilgrimage to Sainte-Thérèse de Lisieux. We all took the train together. That's how I regained my sight. Thanks to a miracle. At least, that's what they used to call me the little miracle.'

'And your Papa, did you hear from him?'

'In the end, he came looking for me. He was an entertainer too. He was a trapeze artist. But he wasn't the sort of guy to take his work seriously. And he had too many women after him. That brought him a lot of problems. Because of his permanent money worries, he decided I should go with him and sing on the streets. People came to listen to me in ever greater numbers. The sous used to pour into the collection box. They'd fall from every side. Even from windows, from apartments.'

'Did you love your father?'

'Yes. Nowadays, I have the means to help him but he's dead.'

Edith was a woman in her prime, full of vitality, but when the old memories were stirred up, it was always the painful ones that surfaced. She carried on, saying that she'd sung after that with Simone, her half-sister.

'We did so many things together.'

Edith was tired. She was relaxed. Perhaps at last she would get to sleep. We suddenly became aware that it was nine o'clock in the morning.

'Christie, you must be shattered. Go back to bed.'

'You need to sleep too, don't you?'

'I'll wait for Loulou. We have a contract to scrutinise. And Théo will be waking up soon. I like us to have breakfast together. I can go and lie down later.

14

This was how, whenever she felt the need to talk, Edith got into the habit of coming to my bedroom every night. It was always about five o'clock in the morning. In any case, from then on I woke up about this time, regardless; subconsciously, I was waiting for her visit. Shortly afterwards, I would hear a slight noise. Then her voice whispering at the half-open door.

'Christie, are you asleep?'

I would get up. 'I've slept, Edith. Don't worry.'

I would go directly to the kitchen, because now I was the one making the tea. The first time, it had been her. But after that, after the first time in the library, she had shown me how to go about it, giving me her instructions. When it was ready, I would take the tray and put it down on the coffee table. Edith would raise her pale face towards me, tired, but smiling. We would burrow into our blankets. She'd wet her lips with a little tea.

'It's excellent. My compliments. I won't say this every time, but it really is perfect.'

'If someone had told me that one day I'd be lucky enough to spend my nights chatting with Edith Piaf…!'

'You think it's a privilege?'

'Can you imagine all those people who would give anything to be in my place?'

'There are very few people with whom I could be myself like this. I feel comfortable with you.' She looked at me steadily. 'You're not looking well, Christie. You need to put some honey in your tea. It will do you good. I'll ask them to buy some for you.'

When she said 'they', she was thinking of Nello, or Danielle Bonnel, the secretary. 'Your parents placed their trust in me when they allowed you to live with me. So I feel a little responsible for your health. At La Frette, you had roses in your cheeks. Now, you're looking peaky.'

'I'm twenty, Edith,' I told her, laughing heartily. 'You aren't responsible for the colour of my cheeks! My parents don't expect that of you.'

'I love them. I don't want to let them down.'

She was quiet for a moment, then sad thoughts darkened her eyes again. I knew her better these days, and I knew that she was often haunted by the memory of Marcelle, the child she'd lost.

'She was blonde.'

'Did you want to have a baby?'

'I was seventeen, you know. I met a man, I fell pregnant. The baby made itself, so to speak.'

Edith explored the memories associated with her youth. At seventeen, she lived in Montmartre, seeking her fortune with Louis, the first 'love of her life'.

'When Marcelle was little more than two years old, I was singing on stage. At a little theatre. As I needed milk for my daughter, I asked the boss for an advance on my wages. He just sniggered. "If you need more, go back to singing on the streets."'

'I replied, "Marcelle is ill. She needs milk." I thought of the good Normandy milk that my grandmother and the girls had given me to drink when I was a little girl, and which had done me so much good.

But this theatre director didn't give a toss that my little daughter was ill. He carried on laughing unpleasantly. I was furious. I shouted in his face, "One day, I'll be a famous singer! I'll sing in music-halls! And you'll be raising the curtain!" Some months later, my poor little Marcelle was dead. And, later again, I became Piaf, the Little Sparrow, then Edith Piaf. And I did sing in music-hall. At the ABC, on boulevard Poissonière. There was tremendous applause. The shouts of 'Bravo!' went on and on. They continued even after the curtain closed. It was a very thick, heavy curtain. And who did I see, working the curtain? My ex-boss…'

'You'd had a premonition.'

'Yes. I could see that he was trying to make himself as small as possible. He wasn't at all keen for me to recognise him. I learned afterwards that he had lost his theatre. He had gone bankrupt. Now, he was at the ABC. He'd fallen back down to the bottom of the ladder. There he was, raising the curtain.'

'What did you think?'

'I said to myself, "We'll sort you out, little man!" In general, I don't abuse curtain calls. I let the audience clap. I ask for it to be opened once, never more. It's not worth it. But in this case, I made him open and close the curtain, again and again. Eight times! The next night, he wasn't there. He had got the point. Someone else had replaced him.'

'You didn't see him again?'

'Never.'

'What age would Marcelle be today?'

'Nearly thirty.'

The subject was still extremely painful for her.

'And your family?'

'It's difficult. I became ill and they stopped coming to see me… I feel lonely. It's weird, after all this success. You are right at the top but you don't have anyone.'

'You have Théo. He's right by your side. You're not alone any more.'

Edith sighed. 'I know. Every second counts a great deal…' An idea came to her. 'Do you think it would bother your parents if I called them? After all, your mother and I are practically the same age. We could have a chat.'

'I'm sure that wouldn't bother them at all. They love you, Edith.'

'They took it badly, didn't they? Accepting our marriage, I mean. They were worried. They must have been telling themselves that their son was marrying an old woman, that he'd never have any children, that sort of thing.'

'Yes, they took it badly. That's the truth. But they understood that you loved Théo. They knew you were happy together. And then…'

'And then what?'

'Instead of distancing Théo from his family, you've done everything to bring him closer. We really appreciate that.' I added, 'What's important is that you love each other, the two of you. You won his heart and he won yours. It's the same as with your public. Sincerity pays off. You yourself have said to me, 'When you're sincere, you win hearts.'

'I said that?'

'Yes.'

'Then I was right.' She smiled sweetly.

'You loved Marcel Cerdan too, very much. Or am I wrong?'

'You're not wrong. My love for him was very intense. A love that possessed me.'

From time to time, she drank one or two mouthfuls of tea, thinking all the while, always allowing her thoughts to trigger memories, some happy, others laden with grief. 'When we left for New York, I believed that the people over there would welcome me as a great star. I told myself that Marcel wouldn't be well-known in America. He was such a quiet man! I even felt put out on his behalf. I was afraid that I was hiding him in my shadow. But when we came off the plane at the airport, he was the one the crowd was there for! Everyone was cheering him. It was a close call as to whether I was the one left out. If you had seen my face! As it turned out, Marcel was famous on the other side of the Atlantic. Boxing is important in the United States, you know... he already had a big name. Imagine, a world champion!'

Admiration shone in her eyes. 'We were good together, Marcel and I. Our personalities matched well and that made me happy. Marcel was a blend of strength and great simplicity. At that time, I loved him more than all the world.'

'He died in an accident, didn't he?'

'A plane crash. One more tragedy in my life.' She shook her head, as if to shake off the old pain. 'There were plenty of other men. Yves Montand, for example. I knew him before he was famous. I encouraged him, guided him, as with Théo today...'

Her Pygmalion side, which she loved to give reign to, went back a long way; it extended her characteristic generosity, her capacity to detect talent in someone else and her desire to cultivate it, like a natural resource that might be lost if not tended.

'I had a lot of admiration for Montand. His perfectionism, his attention to detail. If he wasn't satisfied, he would set to work on his technique as often as it took. That's a sure sign. I knew I had a future star in front of me.'

'And Aznavour?' It was inevitable that I should think of him because he had recently occupied the bedroom in which I now slept.

'Him too: I knew him right at the start of his career. I gave him a hand as well. And he was a hard worker.' She concluded: 'Now he's reached the very top.'

'Were you always attracted to entertainers?'

'Aznavour was a friend. We weren't lovers. But it wasn't just entertainers. One time, it was a rich man. I loved him. Because of who he was not because of the jewels he gave me...'

'He gave you as many as that?'

'I was covered in them! Gold, precious stones. It cost him a fortune. But we didn't spend years together. After we split up, each time I noticed the jewellery he'd so kindly given me, I felt a huge wave of nostalgia. I thought about him once more, about the good times together. In the end, I was so sick of it that I threw the jewels down the toilet! Gold, gems, everything! I pulled the chain.' She shivered. At moments like this, I could sense her need to cling to the present.

'Now, I have Théo.'

'And it's different?'

'It's more that I've changed. I'm capable of a deeper attachment. And then Théo is so tender, so loving. I could almost forget how beautiful he is!' She laughed. 'Our love affair is the sort of story people dream of, while telling themselves it can never happen in real life.'

'You feel secure with him.'

'He protects me. He protects me even against myself. He supervises my regime. He makes sure I get enough rest. And he protects me against the rest of the world. That's the reason we like to stay at home, just the two of us. Snug and warm. Nice and peaceful. You've noticed?'

'Of course.'

'Love, that's what counts the most. Without love, it doesn't work.'

'Without love we are nothing at all, like your song says.'

'And it's true. I need to love to feel I'm alive. To feel I'm a woman. For us women, when we truly love, then yes, we can say we are truly alive.'

'I would like to love the way you do, Edith.'

'You will love.'

‘How will I know it’s love?’

‘You’ll know. You will know it’s true love when you find it.’

She looked at me with her lovely, trusting smile. She really had an extraordinary expression. In one moment, the little girl frightened by the great mystery of life became a woman full of assurance, capable of understanding it all. Everything about her was beautiful, due to her dazzling personality. This was even true of her hands, despite the arthritis which crippled her fingers, a flaw she didn’t try to hide. During these nocturnal conversations, when she opened up completely, she was the very incarnation of passion. She used to sing with all her soul in the same way she loved with all her heart. Love and her gift; those were her priorities. Money counted little for her. She didn’t put anything aside for her old age. Almost as if she knew, in some kind of premonition, and given her state of health, that she wouldn’t have an old age anyway. That was why she spent her money as soon as it came to her. Another thing in common with Théo, among many.

Of course, it was often famous names that came to her lips when she was conjuring up the old days. That of Jean Cocteau, for example. Cocteau – poet, writer, painter, film producer – was at that time an icon for all of Paris at that time. He also figured among Edith’s important friends, even if it was difficult to perceive what brought them together, given the differences in background, culture, personality. If Cocteau was a Parisian bourgeois, Edith was a Belleville Parisian. Cocteau was a universal artist, a multi-talented genius. Edith only knew how to sing.

However, they connected through the profoundly artistic way they looked at their lives and at life in general, and through the search for a kind of beauty. Cocteau was a hand, Edith was a voice; the hand and the voice were in pursuit of the same emotion. In any case, Cocteau saw in her an exceptional person. In 1940, she asked him to write something for her and so *Le Bel Indifférent, The Sound of Silence*, was born. She acted in this modern drama with Paul Meurisse someone to whom she was very close. The performance was a triumph. Its plot was very simple: a cabaret singer lives with a man who is very good-looking, but no longer loves her. The whole play is set in a shabby hotel room lit by neon signs outside in the street. When the man comes back, it's so he can lie on the bed and flick through the newspaper. The woman launches into a passionate expression of her love for him. The man stays mute. At the end, he folds up his paper, gets up and leaves.

For Edith, finishing like this represented the end in the most harrowing sense of the word the door closing on an icy silence. Edith told me that it was the part of the play that hurt her the most. She felt as if the ground had caved in beneath her, she felt overwhelmed by the feeling of abandonment, always so much a part of her, and which was re-awoken by the magic of theatre. The audience was in its turn overwhelmed. If you believe the interviews with Meurisse, Edith was not a great actress but she played her role creditably. And, for good reason, the character embodied something which had always been part of her, which was even one of the driving forces in her life this need for another person, this insatiable need to not be alone.

She chose her friends from the men around her rather than the women – just as she preferred young people to older company. But one of her good friends was Marlene Dietrich. I was surprised at this as the two women seemed like chalk and cheese.

'I like her personality. Obviously, we don't have the same type of physical appearance.'

They were in fact opposites. Edith's charm came from her sincerity, her wholehearted, playful, spontaneous disposition. Marlene, on the contrary, embodied inaccessible mystery.

'When we used to go together to a reception, she would go to the Ladies' Room after an hour. And it wasn't just to powder her nose, Christie, believe me! She would completely re-do all her make-up. When she returned, her incredible beauty would be as if recomposed. I could never have managed that.

It's true that Edith didn't spend much time putting on make-up. A dab of blue eye-shadow, a touch of red lip-stick and the job was done. I never saw her wearing nail-varnish! And for her hairstyle she always kept her natural colour.

'My working-class public doesn't like me to put on airs. One day, my hairdresser gave me a superb cut. He spent ages on it. But I was singing in the rougher suburbs that evening. When the curtain rose, so did the shouting from the audience. "We want our Edith back. Go and get your hair sorted." I went to the wings and brushed out my hair. When I came back on stage, everyone was so pleased that they kept on clapping.'

Nevertheless, she liked to take care with her appearance. Théo gave her two velvet house-coats, really warm and elegant garments. At home, she wore them a lot. He also bought her two babydoll nightgowns, one in sky blue and the other in pink. They were very short nightdresses but she was so slight that they were a normal length on her. She loved everything Théo gave her. She herself never went out to do what today, even in French, is called 'shopping'. It was the boutiques that came to her. All she had to do was choose. And when she'd made her choice, with Théo's help, she would ask me if something took my fancy. I didn't need many toiletries at that time. And that had Edith's approval.

'What's important,' she asserted, 'is what's inside.'

Because, inside, there was love. For her, everything was based on that foundation: feelings, emotions inspired by others, especially by those who suffered. During the Occupation, she went to sing in Germany for French prisoners in the camps. The tour lasted six weeks. At each stop, she asked to be photographed with these unhappy men, forced to live – to survive rather – far from home, far from their families, enduring privations and bullying. Once back in Paris, she took the photos out of her belongings to cut out the faces. Then she made I.D. papers that she took to the prisoners when she went on tour again. She sneaked these papers to the men without letting the authorities see what she was doing. Many men were saved by her actions. I found what she did to be very brave!

'Weren't you scared?'

'I didn't realise the danger. Those boys were so miserable! I had to do something for them.'

Edith liked all men, whatever their nationality. She never got involved in politics. She never gave people her ideas or opinions, just her heart, her affection and her support.

15

That's how I truly came to know Edith in the half-shadow of the library, in that apartment, usually devoted to the noise of visitors and rehearsals, now turned suddenly silent, prompting exchanges and confidences. When I arrived at boulevard Lannes with my belongings, I had an idealised vision of Edith. For me, Edith was Piaf, the superstar whose portrait was posted everywhere, whose life story unfolded in magazines, whose familiar voice came over the radio and echoed in every household. Then we started taking tea together, night after night, and it was the image of a quite different Edith that began to take shape in my mind, that of a woman like other women, tormented by her past, anxious about the future, weakened by illness but still strong from the love she wanted to give others. Most of the time, she didn't mention her poor health: a fever, physical suffering. She regarded her spells in hospital as episodes not worth dwelling on. She preferred talking about Théo. This was the main subject of her existence. Next came work; singing. But singing for her was another way of loving. Love and the stage were two sides of the same coin. In any case, it was with Théo that she performed from that time on.

When they started touring again, I formed part of the couple's intimate circle and it seemed completely natural for me to become one of the troupe. We left for the north – the Netherlands, Belgium. I remember the Amigo Hotel in Brussels where we had an enormous suite, and l'Ancienne Belge Theatre, where the public listened to concerts while drinking beer. Edith and Théo were a huge success but instead of clapping, people shouted out their praise and banged on the tables! Théo could take heart. He had ventured on this tour without knowing whether this new public would accept him, yet the evidence was conclusive. It was true that Edith had worked on his rehearsals intensively. She knew from experience that if the Montands and Aznavours had succeeded it had been down to 'working like crazy'. That was her expression. She meant for Théo to do likewise. But sometimes he gave up, exhausted. Then Edith would push him to carry on; she never let something go. Suddenly, the atmosphere would become tense. Then Edith would tell her husband sweetly, 'Kiss me, you idiot'.

And everything would start again as if nothing had happened.

When they weren't singing, they only went out to answer photo-calls for journalists; numerous magazines displayed feature articles showing them hand-in-hand or kissing each other. But the rest of the time, they were forced to stay at the Amigo because, in town, a horde of admirers followed them everywhere.

As far as I was concerned, it was Edith who pushed me to get out and about, to go and see the way of the world.

'There's no need for you to spend your days locked in your room,' she told me. 'Get out there!'

Then she addressed Francis. 'Wouldn't you like to take her somewhere?'

Francis was only too willing. And Edith never forgot to admonish him, just as we were about to go out, 'You take good care of Christie! I hold you responsible for anything that happens to her! Don't take her anywhere that's not suitable! And don't treat her like you do all the other girls!'

I was a bit annoyed by this behaviour from Edith. In my opinion, she tended to try too hard to protect me, on the pretext that she didn't want to let my parents down. Francis was ten years older than me and I don't believe he'd have risked putting me in danger. He could tell that I felt a bit lost in this new life, this environment so completely different from what I'd known, and it was important to him too that he watched over my safety. We would go for a walk through the network of streets, eat at a restaurant, have a drink.

At the hotel, the troupe had settled into old habits. Edith had a weakness for dining 'at home' and, seeing as she was following a strict regime, liked to eat in her suite after the concert. Danielle, the secretary, was in charge of the meal, which she prepared in the bathroom on a camping stove. Danielle was married to a musician in the troupe. She always created the same menu: minced beef with rice or pasta, a bit of gruyère cheese, peaches in syrup for dessert. When her plate was served, Edith would grab the pepper-mill and give it generous turns over her food.

After Brussels, we left for Liège. You could say that everywhere Edith and Théo went, success followed them. Their posters were plastered all over the walls, the papers talked of nothing else, journalists laid siege to our hotel. The other country that was impatient to see them was the Netherlands. I remember a vast theatre decorated in an ancient Greek style. When Edith appeared , the audience rose as one man, and the cheers resounded like an enormous thunderclap. Then, because the Dutch were such disciplined people, she sang in a silence that was almost religious. After the Netherlands, the tour reached Germany, where the same was repeated each time: we would settle into the hotel; the packs of reporters would head along the pavement as far as the hotel reception, with cameras and all their photographic gear; and the next day, the couple Edith Piaf- Théo Sarapo would be on the front pages of all the papers. Edith was worshipped across the entire planet as the incarnation of French realist *chanson*. This was the case in Greece, in Italy, in Spain, in the U.S.A. And her life, her love affairs, her health and her pain fed a permanent spectacle which the public devoured. After her return to France, concerts followed on the outskirts of Paris. Then Edith invited all her troupe to a top restaurant where she managed to order her favourite dish, the famous eel with spinach and herbs.

As Christmas approached, Théo asked Danielle to take Edith off somewhere, on whatever pretext. Edith feigned shock but she wasn't duped; she realised that her husband was preparing a surprise for her. Indeed, he had cooked up the whole idea with Nello. After Edith and Danielle left, Théo and Nello went in the Mercedes to fetch a giant fir tree which they carried back to the library. It was enormous the tip touching the ceiling. Théo festooned garlands of lights on it. I helped him finish decorating with baubles and multi-coloured stars. Then we stepped back to admire the effect. The sparkling Christmas tree stood out against the red velvet lining the walls. Having disappeared for a minute, my brother came back with a cuddly toy. It was a huge teddy-bear, bigger than Edith. Théo put it at the foot of the tree, saying, 'I tried to find the most beautiful teddy-bear for her that has ever existed. That will make up for all the ones she never had when she was little.'

A noise could be heard in the hallway. Edith and Danielle were back. At once Théo went to fetch Edith and, taking her by the hand, led her into the library. Edith was expecting something, as I've said, but she had never imagined the Christmas tree and the gigantic teddy-bear. I saw pure joy lighting up her blue eyes. For the space of a second, Piaf was turned into a little girl full of wonder. At the same time, it was difficult for her to process the shock. Straight away, Théo took her in his arms and murmured in her ear, 'Happy Christmas.'

'Happy Christmas,' replied Edith, in a voice trembling with emotion. And she added, lightly, to try and control her feelings, 'Now, that's what I call a proper Christmas!'

Théo had thought of everything. A moment later, all the employees were there so that they too could wish Edith a happy Christmas. I was among them. Each of us had a little present for her. We exchanged kisses and hugs. Edith was brimming with joy. She kept saying, 'This is the most wonderful Christmas I've ever had. A proper Christmas with a splendid tree!'

She had a present for her husband. An electric train set! This had a story behind it too, linked to Théo's childhood. It dated back to the time when we still lived in Paris, on rue de Provence. One day, the neighbour from below came to see us. She had brought an electric train for Théo. She explained to Maman that her own son had grown older and no longer played with the set. Why shouldn't another child benefit? For months, Théo had a marvellous time playing with this toy dropped from heaven. Then the neighbour came to reclaim it. My brother was inconsolable for a while but he finally came to terms with his disappointment. The episode did leave its mark on him, though, to the extent that he'd recounted it to Edith. And Edith, who didn't forget her husband's confidences, had come up with the idea of giving him an electric train for Christmas 1962 – their first Christmas together.

In essence, the same intention had crossed both of their minds. Both of them had wanted to fill a gap Théo to compensate for the Christmas trees that Edith had never had, and Edith to heal the wound from Théo's childhood.

16

During the winter of 1962-63, Edith had the idea of suggesting that I be a guest singer in the spectacle that she and Théo were going to perform. They were preparing for a new tour and she imagined that I would be able to play a part. No doubt she was also saying to herself that I needed something to do. It was time, in her eyes, that I started working. She knew that Papa had asked me to come back to La Frette from time to time and help in the hairdressing salon when they were swamped and that I'd never actually taken up this invitation. I didn't miss La Frette one bit. I was far from unhappy in my new life. Especially when I'd had the privilege of travelling in the Netherlands, in Germany, sleeping in the best hotels, frequenting top restaurants. But it is true that a young girl should have something to do...

During the same period, when she found me at a loose end one afternoon, Edith said, 'I would like to hear you sing.'

Soon after that, she turned to the others – Théo, Francis and Loulou. 'Leave us. I want to listen to

Christie's voice and I don't need you all under my feet.'

She wasn't in the habit of wearing gloves when she addressed her entourage! I have no idea what the three accomplices got up to, whether they went for a drink or something, but I found myself alone, in a situation I wasn't used to and one that was very different from our nocturnal exchanges. This was another Edith. This was Piaf the professional. She had caught me off guard and I felt intimidated.

'Sing something for me, Christie.'

I don't remember any more what I sang for her. No doubt, some song that was running through my head because I'd heard it on the radio, because she stopped me straight away with these words, 'I prefer songs whose words have meaning.'

The fashion was for yé-yé music. That's what we called the songs in vogue with young people in the 1960s. Their marketing was assured by *Salut les Copains*, a magazine with a wide circulation which, the following summer, would celebrate its first birthday by reuniting two hundred thousand youngsters at the Place de la Nation in Paris. The expression yé-yé designated songs almost always inspired by American entertainment. It was typical of that era when many singers – Johnny Halliday, Hugues Auffray, Dick Rivers – successfully adapted tunes from across the Atlantic. The yé-yé singers were numerous and held an important place in the everyday life of the under-thirties, who aspired to a more casual existence than that of preceding generations. These artists included Sheila, Frank

Alamo, Richard Anthony, Nino Ferrer, France Gall and Françoise Hardy, Eddy Mitchell and Sylvie Vartan. However that might be, Edith preferred more traditional *chanson*, which told a story. She liked Brel, Bécaud and Brassens. She carried on, 'Apart from that, you don't have such a bad voice.'

She added, 'I will write some songs for you. And I'll get you to work on some numbers that I sang when I was young.'

Decidedly, I was going from one surprise to another!

Un garçon chantait
Une fille pleurait

(A boy was singing
A girl was weeping)

I started to rehearse the song at boulevard Lannes, under her direction, all afternoon. Francis accompanied me on the accordion. Edith kept to what she had decided; she brought out old numbers with me in mind or she wrote new ones for me. Next, she behaved with me as she had with Théo: I had to work really hard.

This period was notable mainly for us preparing for the forthcoming recitals but there was one amusing event when Edith set herself up as chief organiser for a concert at La Frette in honour of Théo's birthday. I thought this was a great initiative and Théo immediately proclaimed to the idea as 'tremendous'.

'Everyone over there will be really pleased to see me again,' he said.

He immediately called our parents and informed them of the plan. 'We're coming to La Frette to celebrate my birthday. At Christie's school.'

Papa replied that he would go straight away and ask for an interview with the mayor to see what he thought.

Théo closed with, 'Tell him the proceeds will go into school funds.'

In those days, La Frette was a community of about fifteen hundred inhabitants where no-one could be unaware of the link between the Lamboukas and the great Edith Piaf. The hairdresser and his family were well-respected and loved. In most cases, even if people remained discreet when they saw the white Mercedes parked in front of the garden gate, they were proud of the celebrity status acquired by their little town. As expected, the mayor gave his assent; the famous recital would take place on the 26th January in the school we had attended as children.

In the meantime, we went back to La Frette one Sunday: Edith, Théo, Francis Lai and me. It was Edith who insisted that Francis should come with us, as she intended to sing 'for Papa and Maman', to use her words.

'I will perform *Non, je ne regrette rien*. I need someone to accompany me. Would you like to come, Francis?'

'They love that song,' Théo emphasised.

Edith sang that day in the family living-room. Francis took his place on the edge of an armchair, his accordion on his knees. He ran his fingers over the first chords. The famous voice, unmistakeable amongst all others, filled the room. My parents were overcome with emotion.

Ni le bien qu'on m'a fait
Ni le mal
Tout ça m'est bien égal.
Non, rien de rien...

(Not the good that I've known
Not the bad that I recall
It's all the same to me.
No, nothing at all...)

At the end, we all clapped as if we'd just heard the song for the first time.

'Thank you, thank you,' Edith repeated. She had put all her heart into it. 'I'm glad you enjoyed it.'

'I'd like to do something for you in return,' Maman told her. 'Tell me something that would bring you pleasure.'

Edith and Théo exchanged looks. She was reluctant to say what she really wanted. Théo gently encouraged her, giving her a kiss. Then Edith said, 'I've always dreamed of wearing woolly gloves. Hand-knitted gloves.'

Maman smiled. 'I will knit a pair for you. What colour would you like them to be, your woolly gloves?'

'I'd like blue ones,' Edith replied. 'To match my eyes. Seeing as you've always told me I have nice eyes.'

The two women shared an understanding that was strengthened after our parents had expressed their fears over the future of their son. Having crossed one big hurdle together, they had grown close. However that might be, the deal was done. All that remained was to drink a cup of tea and eat cakes from the best pastry-maker in Cormeilles.

The 26th January soon arrived. La Frette was turned upside down. The police had deployed back-up and most of the streets were closed to traffic. All the tickets had been reserved ages ago and the school hall was under surveillance by the gendarmes. Reporters had arrived by the score. At all of the crossroads you came across were those who had not yet been named 'paparazzi', as well as television technicians. The residents happily answered the journalists' questions. Anticipation built up, everyone waiting for the arrival of the white Mercedes carrying Edith and Théo. I was in it with them. The car was awkwardly parked in front of our house; the crowd, bristling with microphones and cameras, was so enormous that Nello couldn't manage to carve a way forward. From time to time, he would open a window and say to the journalists, in the hope of making them see reason, 'M and Madame Sarapo will give a press conference at the school hall.'

He behaved according to his instructions from Edith and Théo but it was a lost cause; neither the reporters nor the curious onlookers were willing to beat a retreat so easily. Everyone wanted to see the most famous couple of the year, and to take a photo of them for the magazines, or just to keep as a souvenir.

At home, our parents had prepared a generous reception, with petits fours and unlimited champagne. A huge tiered cake held pride of place in the lounge, topped with the inscription, 'Happy

Birthday, Théo!' And Maman was busy knitting the famous blue gloves... She hugged Edith, saying, 'I've almost finished them, I've only got the thumb left to knit. But you must be in a hurry to get to the school hall.'

Edith wanted to underline the importance of the present in her eyes. 'I will wait till you've finished. I'd like to wear them when I go out to sing.'

A few minutes later, I saw Edith slip on the blue gloves and look at them with an air of satisfaction, like a little girl who's just been given a present. She hugged Maman. After the reception, when we were all heading off in the direction of the school, she kept admiring her hands in their blue gloves, and showing them off to Théo – who was both happy and nervous, for a prophet is without honour in his own country, and to come back and sing in the little town where he'd lived for so long was not the easiest of challenges. We kept coming across faces we half-recognized, and sometimes very familiar ones. At the school hall, we were welcomed by the mayor, with police officers surrounding him. The mayor thanked Edith at length and told her how much he admired her. He greeted Théo as a local hero. He even thanked me for coming too. He was very honoured by the gift we were offering that day to his community.

However, I was more intimidated than ever. It had been agreed that I would open the festivities by announcing the programme: Théo Sarapo as support act and Piaf as the star. I would also sing three numbers, exactly as Edith had decided.

It goes without saying that the school hall was full to bursting. How could it hold so many people? The audience was sitting on all sorts of chairs, none matching, brought together for the occasion from all four corners of the town. There were even garden loungers! But many spectators were standing, or perched on the sills of high windows. I was emotional at seeing the dais where I'd once danced the minuet with my classmates, a long time ago, dressed up as Marie Antoinette. I remembered that it was a rickety dais, likely to fall apart when several people jumped on it at the same time. We stayed in the wings. Even though the black curtain was still closed, if I moved it aside a little, I could see my old school-mates. They were laughing like mad, just as they used to do in class!

Then, suddenly, the black curtain opened. How strange it was to perform in front of these rows of familiar faces! I was unsettled to the extent that I forgot my words. A complete blank! I had to improvise. Nobody seemed to notice. My performance was given thunderous applause.

But that was nothing compared to what the audience had in store for Théo and, of course, Edith. I waited till there was calm once more. I announced the programme to follow. Théo came on in his costume. He too found it bizarre to sing in front of the residents of our small town, gathered here, and to have in front of him the friends with whom he used to perform amateur theatre. But this rather special audience was happy at my brother's success, and at the incredible adventure he was living at that time, someone who'd started off in the hairdressing school of Chantoiseau, before marrying Piaf and finding his direction in variety shows.

When it was Edith's turn to come out on the dais, the people who'd found a perch on the window-sills began to bang on the tiles. The noise was deafening. And, as was customary, it stopped like magic the moment Piaf's voice rang out. Of course, on that special day, she made sure that she called her husband to her side; one more time they sang their now-famous duet, the aptly named *A quoi ça sert l'amour, What is the point of love?*

After the spectacle, we made our way back to my parents' house with great difficulty. Thank goodness we had help from the police! Lots of journalists were waiting there for us, gathered around the tiered cake, impatient to raise their champagne glasses. But the atmosphere was completely different from that of music-hall, where the tensions are almost always perceptible. Here, the prevailing mood was typical La Frette, provincial and easy-going. People were friendly, attentive, playful, delighted with what they'd seen and heard. Many of the reporters there that day were to become friends in our eyes. After taking their photos and recording their interviews, they were more than willing to let us dine peacefully as a family. The meal finished with singing, everyone joining in a choral rendition of 'Happy Birthday' for Théo around the candles lit by Papa, the flames flickering in the darkness. Théo had just carried off a big occasion. Edith was surprisingly calm. The link between her and our family was cemented once and for all.

The next day, at Place de la Gare, the news kiosk was covered in advertising posters printed by the popular magazines, showing the couple Edith Piaf-Théo Sarapo at La Frette. Huge headlines proclaimed, 'They've won everyone's heart at La Frette, all over the little suburb.' I don't need to tell you that all the papers, all the magazines available that day sold like hot cakes, with the newsagent having to order more copies by the boxful to satisfy the demand. In the weeks that followed, Edith and Théo received an endless stream of thank-you letters from the residents of La Frette.

As my own birthday falls in February, the celebrations began again just a few days after the events at La Frette.

'Twenty-one is a very important birthday!' stated Edith.

A crowd of visitors invaded boulevard Lannes. In addition to Edith and Théo, and people I knew thanks to them, there were my parents, my sister and some relatives. Théo gave me a beige fur coat in luxury Indies sheepskin. I opened Edith's present: a Cartier watch! My parents had bought me a locket inset with multi-coloured stones. Even dear Francis Lai had something for me: a satin scarf which he presented to me, warmly wishing me 'a lovely life'. Francis proved to be a very generous man, whose company I enjoyed.

Of course, the champagne flowed like water, and I too had the right to a cake – a masterpiece in white, a huge confection topped with a festive 'Happy Birthday, Christie!'

Following all this, despite my 'failure' at the school hall – albeit a fiasco that no-one had even noticed – I started rehearsals again with Edith and was gaining confidence. And, as she never lost sight of her objectives, she said to me one day, 'I want you to be in our next tour. And for you to announce the concert with Sophie in your arms.'

Sophie was a poodle that Théo had given her. Everyone loved the idea.

That was how I ended up one fine evening once more treading the boards – and not in the school hall at La Frette this time, but in a real theatre.

This time I was the one who'd become a variety artist.

Edith and Théo had decided to put on the show in Bobino in February, then in different towns throughout France. Obviously I remember my first stage appearance at the theatre in Chartres, and my anxiety when, having peeked through the curtain, I discovered stalls black with people, an ocean of bodies, of coats, of strangers' faces. And that incessant murmur, punctuated with exclamations and laughter. We were only a few minutes from the opening and I was paralysed with stage fright. What could I do to forget the presence of all those people? Théo must have felt the same way on his first time, I told myself, and yet nowadays he was so relaxed when he came on stage, like a born performer. He had even sung at Olympia! But for all my attempts to reason with myself, my legs were shaking, my mind was blank and my stomach was in knots. Luckily, Edith was nearby. She held my hand. She whispered, 'It'll be fine, Christie.'

She was very calm, confident, smiling. And her attitude gave me the strength I needed. We went back to the wings. Edith hadn't let go of my hand. Théo put Sophie in my arms.

The next second, the lights dipped in the hall, while silence fell little by little. The curtain rose. Edith gave me a little push, telling me quietly, in English, 'Go!'

When I returned to the front of the stage, my legs could hardly carry me. But as soon as I found myself facing the audience, a different Christie was born. I stared into the darkness of the auditorium. Right at the back the 'Exit' signs were glowing. I glanced briefly at the line of faces in the front row. Suddenly, I felt strong.

I began by presenting Sophie, Edith's poodle, to the audience. She was behaving perfectly in my arms. After that, I announced the programme. At that time, music-hall spectacles always offered a very varied programme: an opening number, trapeze acts and comedians, a guest singer, an interlude, and, finally, the second half reserved for the great star. After this brief appearance, I took Sophie back into the wings, while the orchestra laid into the opening bars. I was quickly back in the lights to deliver the three songs that Edith had written for me. At the end of the third number, the audience applauded me! I was astonished and so happy. I didn't want to leave the stage.

Off-stage, Théo and Edith opened their arms to me. They were all smiles.

'How do you feel?' asked Edith.

'I didn't want to stop!'

'What did I tell you?'

I saw by her expression that she knew exactly how I felt. The orchestra carried on playing. Acrobats clad in white leapt across the boards. A couple with a bicycle followed on. Then a comedian. And, once more, it was my turn to go back on stage, this time to announce my brother's act.

'And now we have... *Théo Sarapo*!'

The audience stood up amid thunderous cheers. Women were shouting, 'Théo! Théo! We love you!'

Théo acknowledged them, thanked them with a smile. He was wearing his black outfit, so expressive. You could see the way happiness radiated from his features. In the wings, Edith and I were holding hands. She had prepared a jug of water and a glass for him. Between numbers, during the applause, Théo joined us, took a mouthful of water and exchanged a kiss with Edith. Then he went back in front of his public, with that same modest manner; he had something about him of a child in a sweet shop but his performance was perfect.

After Théo's slot and the interlude, I went back on stage one last time to announce Edith Piaf. The audience was on its feet before the orchestra even played the first notes, before the singer even appeared in that little black dress which was the perfect counterpoint to Théo's outfit. The robe blended into the shadows. All you could see of Edith was her face and the hands placed on her hips. Then her voice rang out, filling the theatre.

Just as at Olympia in the autumn, the highlight of the spectacle came when, interrupting her recital, Edith turned to the wings and asked Théo to join her in the spotlight and to sing the duet with her, *À quoi ça sert l'amour?*

This successful tour was scheduled for different towns throughout France, and I made the acquaintance once more of the itinerant life I'd led in the previous season in Belgium, the Netherlands and Germany. The difference was that from now on I was a member of the troupe. That troupe to which I tried to belong by getting along with everyone, by trying to be myself, most of all to divert attention from the fact that I was Théo's sister and Edith's protégée.

Edith and Théo were so popular that people even came to greet them at restaurant tables.

'Monsieur and Madame Sarapo!' they would say. 'We think you're great!'

Sometimes, the couple was a little irritated by these demonstrations, but it was the rule to always remain friendly and affectionate towards the public, not because Edith was afraid of losing fans, but because it was important to her that she came across as a person like any other, she who had been both pilloried and rewarded by life in extreme measures.

In each town, Edith and Théo had a suite, retained by the tour organisers, which always included a room for me. It was important to them to keep me close. Edith might have wanted to make me independent, but she continued to feel responsible with regard to my parents. She was seeking the right balance for the young girl she'd taken under her wing, and whose shyness was gradually disappearing.

However, I remained very innocent. Yes, I came on the stage each evening to sing in front of a large audience, but my reactions could still be those of a child. During one stop between two towns where we were supposed to perform, it was impossible to reserve a luxury suite and Edith took me to one side. 'Christie, this hotel doesn't have a suite. You'll have to be on your own in a room...'

'No problem, Edith. I'm twenty-one! I can sleep on my own!'

'In any case, I don't want you to worry, you'll be on the same floor as us.'

'No, *I'm* the one who doesn't want *you* to worry; nothing's going to happen to me.'

It was two o'clock by my watch when the groans made me wake with a start. The moaning came from the room just beneath mine. A woman must be really ill, in need of help. I thought of the pain I felt myself once a month, enough to make me cry like that sometimes. By now I had fully woken up. I was racked with anxiety. I got out of my bed. Throwing a blanket over my shoulders, I picked up the phone to dial Reception.

The receptionist on night duty answered me in sleepy voice. I informed him that groans were reaching me from the floor below. The man asked for my room number. I gave it. And I insisted, 'It's a woman. She's ill. You should take her a hot-water bottle and a cup of tea.'

The receptionist left a long pause, and then allowed himself to say, 'If the lady needs a hot-water bottle, she'll call me herself to tell me. Don't worry about it. I really don't think this woman is ill.'

How heartless, I thought, hanging up! How could anyone be so selfish? He couldn't be bothered to put himself out, and that was all he cared about! But the groans stopped soon after that, and I managed to get back to sleep. However, a short while later, they started again, waking me up once more. I switched on the bedside lamp. I checked my watch. It was now nearly four o'clock. The moaning grew louder and louder, faster and faster too, and seemed to reach a death rattle…

All at once, I understood what was going on. And I could feel myself going bright red up to my ears, even though I was all alone in my room, without anyone there to judge me or make fun of my naivety. Suddenly, my hand went to my mouth as I realised, 'And I called the night receptionist because of that! I even woke him up! My God! What does he think I am? Will he tell Edith and Théo?'

It was impossible to get back to sleep again: it was only at dawn that I managed to get some rest. After my shower, I went to the dining-room for breakfast. The moment I stepped into the doorway, everyone turned to look at me, smiling: the waiters, the musicians in the troupe, Edith, Théo. When I reached the table where Edith and Théo were eating their breakfast, all eyes were still on me and I felt as if something was amiss. I sat down beside Edith.

'Did you sleep well?' she asked lightly.

'Yes, thank you.'

I was served with a cup of tea. Edith carried on, 'It seems you called the night receptionist?'

Then I understood that everyone in the hotel knew of my interference. 'A woman was moaning. I thought she was having a really bad time of the month. I wanted to get help for her, that's all.'

Edith turned to Théo.

'I don't believe it! Is your sister still a virgin or what?'

'How would I know,' replied Théo. 'I don't check up on her all the time.'

'She can't stay that way!'

Edith continued with some pleasantries, laughing openly. 'Have you decided to ruin my reputation, Christie?'

Then, seeing that I didn't know how to react, 'We'll have to find someone for you.' She added, addressing Théo, 'Someone who won't hurt her.'

In the days that followed, while the tour continued on its way, the affair became the focus of banter between Edith and me. I would ask her opinion. 'What do you think of that one?'

'Not nice enough.'

'And that one?'

'Too old.'

'That one?'

'Too flippant.'

'That one?'

'No way! He's not good enough for you.' And Edith would continue on a more serious note, 'If you want to develop as a singer, Christie, you need to fall in love. How can you sing about love if you don't know what it is?'

In the end, she would conclude with a sigh, 'Well, we'll just have to find someone for you.'

Such was her conception of life: the physical, the emotional and the artistic, all intermingled. She sincerely believed that I would be a better singer once I had 'known' love. Since I had shared her life, and that of Théo, she had done everything to help me become independent, to get me on the right track and make my own way in life. She had begun by offering me a professional stepping-stone through letting me come on stage, and now she thought to complete her work by helping me to find emotional and sexual fulfilment. And what was really irritating for me was that she didn't hide her feelings on the subject. All the musicians in the orchestra were up to date with Edith's views on my private life, and I often caught them looking at me with knowing smiles.

Whenever we were alone, she renewed the attack. 'Well? Have you thought about it? Is there a man you fancy? Which one?'

It was extremely stressful. I wasn't particularly attracted to one man more than another in the troupe. I was happy as I was! But Edith had a huge influence on me and, when she broached the subject, it was impossible to reply along the lines of, 'No, I don't fancy any of them.' So I amused myself by throwing out names, as if for fun. At each name, she would deliver her judgement, always a negative verdict. She found me 'too good' for a date with whichever musician or technician, and so it continued. And those who would have been just right were, unfortunately, 'not available'. The list ended up rather long, and we had not made any progress at all because no suitable candidate had been chosen. Eventually, the little game came to an end. This was fine by me, given that I sometimes found it disagreeable. But, as it turned out, Edith did have a suggestion. She came out with it one day when we were chatting, just the two of us. 'Francis.'

Francis Lai was someone I liked very much. He paid me a lot of attention and took me to explore the towns where the tour stopped. However, he had never crossed the limits of friendship, nor given any sign that he'd even considered such a thing. Edith thought he was just behaving as a 'good boy'. In any case, he was the right man for the job.

'Don't you think so, Théo? Francis. He would be just right for Christie. Don't you think?'

Théo had decided not to take these little schemes seriously. He wanted me to lead my life the way I thought best, without interference. On the other hand, he loved Francis as a musician and a friend, and the notion of me being his partner could not be a bad idea.

17

At Bobino, in February, I carried on performing in the spectacle – without Sophie from then on. I announced the programme and sang my three songs, a performance which made me very happy.

Edith and Théo were very successful. The tour had allowed them to move their concerts all around the country. The only problem was the state of Edith's health. She had weakened considerably in the last few weeks. To cap it all, there was an incident in the Dreux stop during the tour; Edith had to cancel her slot and be transported back to Paris, urgently. However she continued bravely in her own sweet way, between daily injections administered by her nurse, rehearsals, moments of privacy with Théo and then her public each evening. Before Bobino, she'd prepared me, 'You'll see, the theatre-goers here are really warm and friendly.'

Before going on stage, she had to take an aspirin. 'It relaxes me,' she said. 'And it's good for my voice.' Saying that, she drank her glass of water. 'So I can swallow the pill.'

Everyone remarked on how exhausted she was. Even the journalists that she was willing to meet were worried for her. They could see our apprehension. In fact, Edith herself was the first to wonder whether she might collapse on stage in front of her public. She asked her doctor for help. Ever the true professional, she was determined to respect the contract she'd signed and to do that she needed stimulants. She tried to take them without Théo knowing, but he wasn't fooled. Taking the doctor to one side, he asked anxiously, 'What's going on?'

'She's under too much pressure. She needs to take a break.'

'I don't want her taking drugs.'

The doctor sighed and looked apologetically at Théo. The state of his patient worried him greatly but he had very little room for manœuvre. As a matter of fact, he was trapped between the imperatives of science and the singer's demands as she clung to her vocation with all her might in her bid to stay alive – and on stage. But her system, and especially her liver, were seriously affected, and we knew that she was walking shakily along the edge of a precipice.

Théo and the doctor decided that she would only take sugar and vitamins, a remedy which, I remember, came in the form of white pills. Unfortunately, these famous white pills had no effect whatsoever. The whites of Edith's eyes were turning yellow. Her features puffed up. She felt exhausted. She needed to be prescribed something stronger. From then on, the nurse would give her an injection each evening before the concert. Frightened, I couldn't help asking the question burning on my lips, 'Are you drugging her?'

'It's not drugs. Don't worry, Christie.'

But Edith even had problems with her voice, which was also starting to betray her. This phenomenon couldn't help but aggravate our worry, and she felt obliged to reassure us. 'My voice is fine. When I'm tired, I force syllables a little, that's all. Don't let it worry you.'

Every evening, in the theatre at Montparnasse, which had witnessed so many great performers, she waited backstage, sitting on a chair, until it was time to make her entrance. A few minutes later, she was singing and it was a different Edith displayed to the world, an Edith transformed. It was an act of great courage to complete this series of concerts. And her last appearance is entered in the annals: a twenty minutes standing ovation for a Piaf exhausted, but still standing upright at the edge of the stage, hands crossed behind her back, eyes fixed on her much-loved public, then a good hour spent in her dressing-room to receive praise from an interminable stream of friends and admirers.

Bobino drained her strength completely and she stayed in her room most of the time. The doctor came to see her every day. As for Théo, he stopped speaking, his face masked permanently by anxiety.

Of course, our nocturnal tea parties had come to an end. But one morning, towards ten o'clock, I headed for the library. The shutters were closed, the room was plunged in darkness. I saw a vague shape hunched up in one of the armchairs. It was Edith. Her eyes were open but she seemed to be elsewhere and the whites of her eyes were yellow. Gripped with fear, I called Danielle.

'Edith isn't well.'

'I know. She's in a hepatic coma.'

'We need to call the doctor!'

'The doctor has been. He said not to disturb her.'

'But the closed shutters?'

'I suppose that too much light might do more damage to her.'

Suzanne came into the library saying, 'No, it's not that. It's Monsieur Théo. He's asked us to keep all the shutters in the house closed.'

Danielle and I were surprised. Suzanne explained, 'Because of the journalists. Monsieur wants to make them believe there's nobody here. We have to behave as if Monsieur and Madame have gone away. If the reporters think Madame is here, they'll be at the door non-stop, disturbing her.'

I was more and more worried at seeing Edith in such a state but Suzanne tried to be reassuring. 'Madame has been like this before. She comes through it each time. It lasts one or two days and then it's over.'

The doctor came back a bit later. Having once more examined his patient, he wasn't happy with her condition. We could see that he was hesitating as to which course of action he should take, that he was wondering whether she should go to hospital. Finally, he opted to keep Edith at home, under supervision. As it happened, that same evening, the patient came out of the comatose state that frightened me so much. She was recovering. She was getting better. She was talking to us. As the nurse had popped out for a minute, it was Danielle and I who helped her to have a bath.And, from the next day on,

Théo took her for a short walk in the Bois de Boulogne. It was Edith herself who insisted on going out somewhere. It was true that the doctor had recommended complete rest but she didn't like rest; she only liked action, working, movement, things happening. Inaction roused her anxiety about death.

It was during this period that Théo received a proposition from the director George Franju, who was just about to film *Judex*. Its very dramatic plot told the story of a banker who was being forced by a mysterious upholder of justice to restore stolen goods to their rightful owners. The film would be shot in black and white. This nocturnal work, mysterious and ethical, suited Théo's personality down to the ground. Clearly, it was a big career opportunity. But the decision wasn't an easy one to make. Edith was very frail, she very much needed her husband at her side. For all that, it was she who pushed my brother to say yes to Franju.

'Do it, Théo. It's work. It's good for you. I want you to say yes. Promise me you'll do it.' She really wanted Théo to pursue his career, and a role in a film wasn't an opportunity that came along every day. She also didn't think it was a bad thing for him to be away from the house more. It was true that she needed him but she was mortified at seeming so weak, diminished, at the end of her tether. She argued, 'I have plenty of people around me, Théo. Everything will be fine. And I have Christie. The two of us can go for walks.'

Théo had to be present on set from five o'clock in the morning and he would return to boulevard Lannes late in the evening. During his absence, Edith did everything she could to avoid letting herself go. She got up, took a bath, had her hair done, put her make-up on. We would cross the street to go for a short walk along the woodland paths. In the evening, although she was shattered, she made sure she looked good for her husband's return.

During one of our walks in the wood, she told me, 'I have to make it happen quickly, you understand. I'm not well. I don't have much time left.'

'What are you talking about, Edith?'

'I'm talking about Théo's career. I won't always be here to help him. But as long as I'm still here, I want to push him. I want him to reach the top…'

'Don't talk like that, Edith. You're on the mend. Your health is improving.'

She wasn't listening. She was following her own train of thought. 'I know I'm too hard on him, at times. I put him under pressure. I hate myself for that and yet, at the same time, I know I have to do it.'

This need to give was so powerful in her. It was a fundamental trait in her character. She always wanted to help those she loved, to given them their chance, share with them a little of her good fortune. And this need was multiplied with regard to Théo, the man she'd married when she'd become so vulnerable.

She walked slowly, holding onto my arm. From time to time, she lifted her eyes to the trees which were starting to turn green. She sighed. 'Springtime already.'

Everything reminded her of her obsessions. 'How quickly time passes. I need to sort out a contract for you. You should be making records, Christie.'

'There's no urgency, Edith. For the moment, all that counts is your health. You're on the road back so take care not to tire yourself out too much.'

It was rare that we could walk for so long without being interrupted; other walkers would often recognize Edith. Sometimes, they would pluck up courage to approach her, to speak to her. It was always so they could say something friendly, to congratulate her, to tell her how much they liked her. She always reacted kindly to them. But she preferred it when we walked peacefully along the paths without encountering anybody. Sometimes she'd even speed up if she thought a passer-by might have recognised her.

When we were truly on our own, she could enjoy nature's awakening to the full.

'I should walk more often,' she said. 'It does me good.'

Then the fatigue would return.

'I'd like to go back now, Christie. Have a siesta. Be on my feet when Théo comes home. I'd like to dine with him, if he's not too late.'

That was how she was, always doing everything she could to be as pretty and fresh as possible for her husband's homecoming. Théo would kiss her. He would disappear for a few minutes, just long enough to change into something more comfortable. Then they would go and chat in the library. Edith took great interest in *Judex*. She was happy that Théo had landed a role in this production that suited him so well. She asked him about Franju, about the atmosphere during the shoot. It was the best time of her day. After a while, Suzanne would half-open the door and let them know their meal was ready. Often, Edith and Théo would eat in their room. As for me during that time, I might go and see a film with a friend.

One day when Théo was on the set, Edith made me go into the kitchen. She had an exercise book and ballpoint pen. She sat down and asked me to do the same, saying. There's no-one else here. We won't be interrupted.'

I wondered what was on her mind. She opened the exercise book. 'I want to re-write my will, Christie.'

Seeing my terrified expression, she cautioned me, 'Not one word to Théo.'

And she continued, saying, 'He doesn't know. I want to make him my heir.'

I was very ill at ease at the idea of being a witness to her re-writing her last wishes. I really didn't want to be associated with such an act, even less let her believe that Théo and I wanted to profit from her fortune. I stammered, 'It's too soon to talk about wills, Edith. You have many happy years ahead of you with Théo.'

But, as always, she stuck to her idea.

'You'll see, when I'm gone…'

'I'll see what, Edith?'

'They will all be after Théo like vultures!'

Vultures… what a terrifying word! How could she imagine herself surrounded by vultures? I was naive, always reluctant to see bad in others. Edith, however, knew exactly what she was dealing with in her acquaintances. In any case, she had resolved to manage the problem and lines were already appearing in the exercise book.

She knew perfectly well that Théo was not looking to profit from her in any way and that, on the contrary, he used money he'd stashed away to cover the cost of buying her presents. It's true that Théo was just like her: money wasn't important, money was meant for spending. Edith didn't manage her income personally. She delegated that to Loulou Barrier and Danielle Bonnel, her secretary. She was happy to spend money without keeping a check on it and, when she needed funds, she just asked Loulou, quite simply. The way of life at boulevard Lannes was rather expensive, as Edith was in the habit of inviting friends for dinner. The butcher's bills were particularly extortionate! But Piaf was a superstar and the money kept coming in.

One morning when Théo was shooting with Franju, Loulou Barrier turned up with a smile on his face. 'I've got a contract for the United States!'

'What sort of contract?' Edith wanted to know.

Loulou was already explaining what it was all about.

'It would be for you and Théo. A tour for six weeks. In the biggest American cities.'

At once, Edith thought of Théo. Her blue eyes went dreamy. She so wanted him to know the United States, the country where she'd left so many memories. She so wanted to turn him into an international star. And she would have done anything to take this journey with him.

'What do you think?' continued Loulou, whose expression now revealed some uncertainty.

He was worried about Edith's health; it was the main obstacle to the plan. She was quick to reassure him. 'I can do it, Loulou. I'm going to do it.'

Loulou came back that evening to discuss it with Théo. My brother welcomed the news with enormous enthusiasm. The United States! The United States with Edith! A concert tour in the big cities of America!

'If Edith is doing better, if she feels up to going, then with pleasure...'

'I am doing better, Théo. I'm fine. We are going to have an amazing trip...'

Did she believe her own words? Definitely. In any case, she intended to stay true to her own nature; she wanted things to move forward, whatever the cost.

Loulou took up the thread. 'We'll leave from le Havre. Embark on the *France*. An eight day crossing with all mod cons.'

'Christie will come with us,' added Edith.

And Théo joked, 'A room in our suite, as usual.'

The atmosphere was one of celebration. Edith and Théo kissed each other, as excited as two children at the thought of crossing the Atlantic and singing for the American public.

Then Edith really began to improve health-wise – perhaps the new project stimulated her in the fight to regain her strength. One blessing never arrives alone, as the saying goes, and the shooting for *Judex* came to an end so Théo was able to stay at home from then on.

Loulou brought us news each day. 'I've rented the suite once occupied by General de Gaulle! Will that do you?'

I remember these moments as belonging to a period of optimism, light-hearted and full of charm. Paris became beautiful with springtime, its terraces invaded each evening by carefree people in summer clothes. Edith, who was tired of being cooped up, wanted more than halting walks along the woodland paths of the Bois de Boulogne. She wanted to go out, to go to clubs, to dine in restaurants, to watch films. And Théo was available now. He could easily accompany her, wait on her hand and foot. In fact, there was nothing he liked better, and in spring 1963 the couple Piaf-Sarapo could once more be seen frequenting the best places in the capital. Their arrival at a restaurant would always trigger the same scenario. The waiters would scurry about, the diners would start whispering, expressing their friendly sympathy through smiles and gestures.

Edith felt good with Théo. She was in safe hands. Everyone witnessed her rediscovering the joy of living.

But, one evening, coming home from a restaurant, she realised that Théo was very worried. 'You should have had something else,' he said.

It came out in their discussion that Edith had given in to her little weakness and chosen her menu without worrying about her regime. Having left the table with the beginnings of indigestion, she was now obliged to reassure Théo, 'I'll eat what I like! Besides, I feel better already. It will pass.'

I thought she was right because they reached their room and I heard nothing more.

But, in the small hours of the morning, I was woken by noises. Footsteps echoed through the house, as if people were coming and going. I looked at my alarm clock: six o'clock. I came out of my room at the moment Théo was crossing the apartment with Edith in his arms. I followed them. An ambulance was waiting in front of the building.

I dissolved in tears. Why would Edith destroy herself in this way? Why couldn't she ever respect the dietary constraints prescribed by the doctors and considered to be of vital importance? Nowadays I know that even the strongest individuals have their weaknesses. As well as the consequences of a childhood and youth marked by poverty, Edith had an Achilles heel gourmet food. Having reached this stage in her life, despite being touched by a presentiment of approaching the end, perhaps she wanted to make the most of all that life could still give her, without worrying about a regime or restrictions.

The ambulance disappeared along the boulevard. I still remember that silent departure at dawn, with no siren. Théo had asked the driver to take them to hospital as discreetly as possible. But at lunch-time, the news-flashes on the radio were about Edith, and it was the same on the television: 'Piaf in a coma!' The whole of France knew that she'd been admitted to the Ambroise-Paré Clinic; people were holding their breath, their ears glued to their transistors. In the days that followed, Théo cancelled all meetings so he could be at his wife's bedside. Inevitably, the media laid siege to the clinic, reporters on the look-out everwhere, invading the grounds.

A week after the crisis, Edith seemed to be out of danger once more. The doctors had got her through the episode. As soon as she knew that her health was better and that she was going to recover, her first reaction was to apologise to Théo, promising him, 'I won't do it again.'

But, all of a sudden, things changed. And that same evening, Théo had to convey a painful decision to Loulou Barrier. 'You can cancel the United States, Loulou. We won't be going any more. It's too risky.'

'Let's say we're putting it back to the autumn,' replied Loulou, who never lost his cool. Nor did he lose sight of his objectives.

'Till autumn, then, agreed.'

But Théo wasn't looking that far ahead. He had really been scared after this series of warnings, and all that he envisaged in the immediate future was to rent a house in the country where Edith could truly rest, avoiding not only the stress but also the outings and mad impulses.

'She needs peace and quiet,' he said.

Shortly after that, he announced to Edith that he had found a wonderful property on the Côte d'Azur, at Saint-Jean-Cap-Ferrat.

'A huge property. Ideal for some rest', he added, 'You should avoid seeing too many people, but if you want some friends to stay there's plenty of room. Guests wouldn't be on top of each other.' Théo was more specific, looking at everyone as he spoke, 'There are fifteen bedrooms.'

'Oh!' exclaimed Edith, 'that's far too big!'

But Théo insisted. 'If you really want to recuperate, you need space. If the house is too small, everyone will be on top of you all the time. And besides, I didn't find anything else. Everything is booked already at this time of year.'

It was June. Théo had leased the property until the end of July.

Edith nodded her head with an air of resignation.

They left, taking with them the cooks, the nurse, the secretary and their new chauffeur, Christian – Nello had left Edith's service.

I stayed for a while on my own at boulevard Lannes, in the deserted apartment that no-one visited any more, all the people in music-hall having gone on holiday. I fed myself on baguettes and chocolate, I drank coca-cola. My principal occupation consisted of waiting for news from Edith and my brother. From time to time, my parents invited me to see them at La Frette. I didn't make them beg me to go and share a comforting meal and the warm affection of family life. I also saw it as a chance to bring them up to date on what I had learnt about the situation at Saint-Jean-Cap-Ferrat.

18

It was indeed an immense property, called *La Serena*. This Italian name evoked tranquillity; you might well say that the house fitted Théo's stated aim when he asked for only one thing: peace and quiet for Edith. Besides, he was the one paying the rent.

They'd been there a week when Théo said to me over the phone, 'Edith wants you back. Why don't you come and join us?'

'I'd love to.'

'It's beautiful here. Just wait till you see it.'

The prospect of gazing at the sea was certainly not unpleasant, and anyway I was used to living with them now; it was boring when I didn't see them. What's more my presence at *La Serena* might prove useful because Théo would have to make some trips back and forth to Paris for the dubbing on *Judex*.

'I'll call Loulou,' continued Théo. 'And I'll ask him to get you a train ticket.'

I took the night train from Paris Gare de Lyon. As usual, Loulou had organised a lot of things booking me a place in first class. I was in Nice when I woke up to the extraordinary light of the south. And when

I leaned out of the carriage window, you can imagine my surprise when I saw Francis! He was waiting for me on the platform, wearing blue trousers and a navy blue polo-shirt. He seemed delighted to be there. We fell into each other's arms.

His white convertible Alfa Romeo was waiting for us in front of the station.

I knew that Nice was his home town. As we drove along the Corniche, the twisting road above the sea, he told me that he was staying with his parents for the summer, and that every day he spent time working on songs at *La Serena* because Edith wanted new material for September.

'How is she doing?'

'She doesn't go out of her room much. Now and again, she says she feels better. You'll be able to keep her company when Théo goes back up to Paris. He has to go because of the film.'

'I know.'

La Serena was a huge property: a stone mansion, perched on a hillside, in the middle of pine trees, with a balcony overhanging the bay and the Mediterranean. It also had a swimming-pool and even steps giving access to a private beach. From the terrace, you could see a yellow craft floating on the blue water.

'What's that, Francis?'

'It's Commander Cousteau's capsule – the oceanographic explorer.'

The garden gave off incredible perfumes. To arrive from Paris and find myself in such paradise was a wonderful experience. Francis also told me that Edith and Théo had David Niven for a neighbour, the actor who'd played the famous captain Phileas Fogg in *Around the World in Eighty Days*.

You entered the mansion via a very bright hall, with marbled floor and access to the grand staircase. Furnished with a massive table, the dining-room was adjoined on one side to a kitchen worthy of a top restaurant, and, on the other, a lounge full of bamboo furniture.

Théo had told the truth; there were indeed fifteen bedrooms, split between two floors. Many of them were occupied because Suzanne was there with her daughter, as was Danielle, the nurse Simone Margantin, and Christian, the chauffeur.

I found Edith in her room, busy with some embroidery work. She liked this type of activity. In Paris, she had created a tapestry to decorate the back of a Louis XVI chair.

'It calms me down,' she said. 'And while I'm doing this, I can carry on thinking.'

If she seemed tired and frail, she still found a smile, and you could see the fun sparkling in her eyes. I asked her whether she liked the house.

'Yes, a lot. Théo did the right thing finding a summer bolt-hole.'

She told me about their arrival a week earlier. Christian had come to meet them at the airport. When the Mercedes was approaching the house, Edith and Théo could see that the media had been forewarned: reporters were already camped on the edges of the property! They even gave the couple a welcome of, 'Bravo, Edith! Bravo, Théo!'

But now they're leaving me in peace,' Edith continued. 'They must have realised that I need some rest. I love the scents of the flowers drifting right into the heart of the house...'

A sad thought came to her. 'It's a pity that Théo has to go back to Paris for *Judex*.'

'I'm here, Edith.'

'Thank you for coming.'

In Théo's absence, Edith rested most of the time. She said she had the impression of getting better and better. Although she usually had meals in her room, sometimes she would come down to dinner with us in the grand dining-room, which had an amazing view. Edith didn't like to be alone, even though she needed to avoid over-stretching herself even a little.

I kept her company, in that room where shutters protected her from the heat, where you could always hear the singing of cicadas. Occasionally, Francis came up to join us and all three of us had discussions that could take a professional turn, in the course of which Edith seemed to watch over us affectionately.

I hadn't forgotten that she used to ask me with great insistence what I thought of Francis... it vexed her to see me still on my own. Very well! Her wishes were to be fulfilled. I was no longer alone because we started going out together, Francis and I. He came to *La Serena* every day. He worked most of the time, but we would often take a swim in the pool, where all we had to do was fool around like a couple in love. As soon as Théo came back from Paris, Francis and I left to explore the hinterland in the convertible Alfa Romeo, or to walk hand-in-hand through the winding streets of Nice's old quarter. He was a charmer, a good-natured man, who knew very well how to attract women. Since I'd moved into boulevard Lannes, I'd seen him as a man who changed girlfriends every week and was really only interested in one thing: music. Until now, especially during the winter tour through French towns, he'd been content to take me out for a drink or to see a film. Now, he was in love. And I liked him very much. But was I in love? I don't think so. I was merely delighted at having him in my life because he had such an appealing personality and so much talent as an artist. Also, I needed to feel protected while I was trying to find myself. At the time, it seemed the most natural thing in the world that we should be a couple – a couple born from our little band of friends, musicians, music-hall people. He was a composer and I was aiming to become a singer. We had fun, we had a good time together. And, above all, we had the blessing of Edith Piaf...

Francis loved to show me Nice cuisine, the little restaurants of the region, the remote villages on hillsides, criss-crossed with narrow streets. He introduced me to his parents, extremely kind people who lived near Nice. Seeing these people who lived so simply, breathing the perfumed air, I understood why it was so difficult to adapt to living in Paris for those who were from the Côte d'Azur. Everything here was so peaceful! The air was so pure! Francis's Papa went into the garden to pick a fig for me and that fruit, freshly plucked from the tree, was one of the best presents I have ever been given. During this time, in the kitchen, Francis's Maman was preparing pans bagnats, traditional Nice sandwiches of tuna and fresh local vegetables in olive oil.

'You have to eat, my girl!' she'd say, slicing tomatoes.

She was alluding to my being so skinny. I weighed 51 kilograms! It's true that I wanted to keep my figure. Firstly because my knight in shining armour liked it, but also because I was influenced by Edith, who kept repeating the same advice. 'Don't eat too much or you'll end up fat like Suzanne.'

She pushed me into going for a massage. She and Théo regularly made use of a masseur's services. At boulevard Lannes, Edith had overcome my reluctance and persuaded me to follow their example. When I confessed that I didn't like the idea of stripping to my panties and bra in front of a man, she saw this as confirmation that I really needed to loosen up! She thought my modesty to be over the top. She was even a little shocked by it, given that she herself had been familiar with promiscuity from childhood and during her youth. Once again, I could see how different we were from the circumstances of our family backgrounds. In the end, I accepted the masseur in Paris. I even grew used to him. Perhaps he succeeded in making me more civilised. It was a different one though who was employed at *La Serena*.

From my father I received a strict education which, in a way, had been continued by Edith to take me through to adulthood. She and I trusted each other. Over the last few seasons I had become part of the troupe and now I was profiting from this vacation on the Côte d'Azur in a dream of a villa where my friends turned up. Edith put herself out to help me develop in every way, while I made an effort to fight my shyness, to be worthy of the aspirations she had for me. However, clashes could also arise between us, even if this was a rare occurrence. I still remember the day I made her really angry. It was an afternoon when she wasn't feeling well. She was shut in her room. But there were lots of people at *La Serena*. Journalists at a bit of a loose end had come to keep us company, Francis and me, Edith made it a matter of principle to treat any reporters who might generate some publicity for her well, and in general she asked Loulou to do likewise. That day there was a whole gang of us sunbathing around the pool. At some point, we began to increase the number of dives, the splashing, the shouting, until the noise sounded like children running wild. It was great fun. I wasn't the last to collapse in loud fits of laughter. But Edith could hear everything because her room with its closed shutters was right above the pool. She sent Danielle to tell me that she wished to speak to me. I slipped on my sandals, draped a bath towel round my shoulders and went up to see Edith. I found her in a bad temper. 'Don't you think you're going over the top, Christie?'

'What have I done?'

'You're laughing like an idiot all the time, while I'm here, feeling ill, stuck in bed!'

'You don't feel well?'

'No, I don't feel well and you're making all that noise!'

She was really irritated. I apologised. I felt truly awful at having behaved like a featherbrain and annoyed Edith. Seeing how bad I felt, she ended the discussion, saying, 'Go back down to the pool. But stop all that laughing. It gets on my nerves.'

I went back to find the others at the pool-side, but I no longer felt at all like laughing. Playtime was over.

That evening, Edith came down to dine with us. I didn't say a word at table. I felt stupid and guilty. It was very difficult for me to get over the incident. When someone asked me what was up, it was Edith who replied, 'I got carried away telling her off this afternoon. I shouldn't have.'

I felt a bit better. The cloud lifted. The bond was re-established. Edith knew that I was sensitive and vulnerable; she preferred to admit that she was annoyed over something trivial rather than to see me unhappy for any length of time.

It was during July at *La Serena* that we had news of Claude Figus. He was no longer part of Edith's entourage, as he'd turned up at boulevard Lannes in a state that left no room for doubt: he was abusing dangerous substances. Edith decided it was best to break off all contact. This was why he hadn't been to visit us, even though he was also staying on the Côte d'Azur. Two visitors did arrive, though asking to speak to Edith and Théo. Figus had been found dead in his hotel room in Nice.

'I suspect he's committed suicide,' Théo said.

'In my opinion, it's connected to the drugs he's been taking,' was Edith's comment.

Théo reacted to this loss with great sadness; Claude was the friend who'd introduced him to Edith.

Even in a weakened state, even on holiday, Edith was always determined to nurture our relationship with our family. That was how my parents came to be invited, with my sister, to come for a fortnight to *La Serena*. Edith had phoned them in person.

'I know you're a good driver, Papa, but please take care on the journey!

Papa drove carefully and one fine evening we saw his Simca being parked under the pine trees. I was really moved to see my whole family reunited in this little corner of paradise. As for Edith and Théo, they were happy to see the family under their roof. At first, they came downstairs to dinner each evening to do our parents the honour of dining in their company. But Edith was too weak; it wasn't long before she could only make an appearance for a short while at the end of each afternoon.

Edith could still show her playful nature, though full of smiles in the presence of my parents. She said to them at the beginning of their visit, 'I can't sing anything for you at the moment but just you wait, I will sing for you before you go back home.'

She spent the greater part of her day with Théo. In the morning, she'd take a bath, then Théo would do her hair and we would see them having breakfast on the balcony of their room. Through Loulou as intermediary, Théo never ceased getting proposals for concerts, but he turned down all offers, knowing that Edith needed him. Sometimes, they tried to work a little, or to play something. But, most often, Edith would knit or do embroidery behind closed shutters, because it was so hot, while Théo, in a shortsleeved shirt, would read the paper outdoors, within a few metres of her. The visits continued: David Niven, who called round as a neighbour, the reporters, the actor Danny Kane, who had sung with Edith at Bobino. Noel Commaret, the pianist, also came by with his wife. There was no question but that society came to *La Serena*; Edith couldn't be anywhere without attracting her court around her, whether more or less numerous, composed of friends, admirers or quite simply people who wanted to make contact with her.

It was Papa's idea to organise something for the National Fête Day of 14th July. He and Maman went to Nice and returned with a bouquet of red, white and blue flowers. They gathered together all the house-guests, including the cooks, the secretary and the chauffeur, asking us to wait at the foot of the marble staircase. After a few minutes, Francis turned up playing his accordion, and pulled us all into a farandole, a lively Provençal dance. With him accompanying us, we sang, *Ah! ça Ira*, the chorus of the 'sans-culottes', the revolutionary workers, and the song that had become the symbol of the French revolution, a song that Edith herself had interpreted in *Si Versailles m'était conté*, the film by Sacha Guitry. The music reached every corner of the house, which found itself galvanised out of the silence of a heavy summer afternoon. Suddenly, behind Francis, Papa could be seen brandishing the tricolour bouquet. When the farandole reached the top of the stairs, Edith was standing in her doorway, in a pink nightdress. She was smiling. She exclaimed, 'A party? I want to be in it!'

Théo came up behind her and put his hands on her shoulders. And we were getting closer, singing to the beat of the accordion.

'Ah! ça ira, ça ira, ça ira !
Le peuple en ce jour sans cesse répète...

('Ah! Here we go, here we go, here we go!
This is the day, again we all say...')

Papa and Maman held out the flowers to Edith. They hugged each other. Very emotional, Edith said, 'Thank you, thank you...'

She moved to one side to let us into her room. We invaded her bedroom. Suddenly, she cried out, 'I know whose idea this is, Papa. C'est toi! It's yours!' She carried on calling him 'Papa', but from that day on, they used the familiar 'tu' form of 'you'.

To offer her a present, Papa and Maman had also bought a beautiful silk scarf in Nice. She had received presents galore in her life, but she could recognise a present given with sincerity, one that came from the heart.

'You make me so happy! Now it's my turn.

She clambered onto the bed. Standing, trying not to lose her balance, the beautiful scarf covering her shoulders, she let rip with *Non, je ne regrette rien*, knowing that it was my parents' favourite song.

I really felt that she'd regained her voice. Once more, she was brimming with life. Once more, the Piaf magic was working. All around her, faces glowed with admiration. Edith would have treated us to a complete concert if Théo hadn't gently put an end to the party, saying that she needed some rest.

That same night, Edith dined alone with Théo, then he came downstairs to tell us how well she felt and that she wanted to thank us for the party, which had given her so much pleasure.

In the days that followed, she started to work again, despite constant fatigue, by being very disciplined concerning her regime and her bedtime. As she regained energy, hope spread through the household. In moments like these, everyone said that she was on the mend, that she would get completely better and succeed in her preparations for the concert tour she had in mind for the autumn. Yes, everyone entertained the possibility that she would be seen once more on stage after this rest cure. Perhaps there would even be another attempt at the American tour, which Loulou had wanted so badly.

But when the moment came for my parents and sister to leave, she announced, 'I want to take you to a restaurant. A particular favourite of mine. Their braised rabbit in mustard sauce is absolutely wonderful!'

I saw a mask of pure fear come down over Théo's features. Once seated at the table, could Edith restrict herself to the prescribed regime? What's more, the restaurant she'd mentioned was an hour's drive along little lanes with hairpin bends.

'Edith,' pleaded my brother in a low voice, 'you know this isn't reasonable.'

'Just once, now and then, can't do me any harm… I'll just have a tiny piece of rabbit, no more than that. I promise!'

We all set off in the various cars. It was indeed a good restaurant, where Edith had been to dine on several occasions. Of course, the manager was honoured by this visit. And his rabbit in mustard sauce was definitely prepared exceptionally well. But we all gave a cautious welcome to this dish out of solidarity with Edith, who had promised Théo she'd only have one mouthful. And no-one dared order dessert. This meant that the meal finished in a slightly tense, if not miserable atmosphere. We feared the consequences.

What followed was so predictable; the next day, Edith had an attack of acute indigestion. In her case, such indigestion had every chance of becoming a hepatic coma. Théo and Simone, the nurse, already thought it best to take the patient to Nice as an emergency. But for once, fate decided otherwise, and Edith recovered very quickly without passing into a dangerous comatose state. Then my parents and sister left. Edith returned to work with Théo, Francis and Commaret. She even wrote some songs for me, for she never lost sight of the idea that I should make a recording as soon as possible. Once more she was at home to journalists, some of whom had taken up residence at *La Serena* for several days. From one moment to the next, the house echoed to the sound of the laughter that made us all so happy. The downside of this good mood returning was that Edith, forgetting all her good resolutions, started demanding the dishes that were forbidden to her. Simone objected but Edith defied her and stated, 'I bet you that I *can* eat this excellent omelette!'

Simone was compelled to call Théo to comme to the rescue, but his intervention was no more successful; now that Edith was feeling better, she had decided to do exactly as she pleased. After the omelette, it was paella, and then, inevitably, the acute indigestion, hepatic coma and hospital in Nice for a whole week – a week during which Théo stayed at her bedside twenty-four hours a day.

19

For the month of August, Théo had chosen a different place to rent; a house at Mougins, a superb village situated further to the west and slightly inland. In his view, there were too many friends and colleagues coming to *La Serena*, and these incessant visits were disturbing Edith's peace and quiet. He thought it crucial to ensure complete rest for her, as he felt that she was growing weaker, even if she seemed to be recovering at times. And, indeed, Edith did have a fairly calm life at Mougins. Loulou came by frequently, but the stream of visitors and journalists had diminished. I did my best to make myself useful around Théo and Simone, the nurse. A certain unease ruled over the new residence. We had the feeling that Edith was finding it more and more difficult to get any rest. She only left her room to stretch out on a lounger in the garden, where she complained of the heat. She didn't work. She didn't have the energy for it. She didn't speak any more about her plans for going on stage in the autumn, even less about the American project, which seemed to have sunk without a trace.

Occasionally, I escaped from this heavy atmosphere. Leaving Edith to the tender care of Théo and Simone, I threw towels and a swimming-costume into a basket, then jumped into Francis's convertible and we headed for the sea. But neither he nor I was really at peace; a premonition of doom hung over all of us who lived in the singer's entourage.

The stay at Mougins was in any case to finish at Le Méridien clinic. Edith had fallen into a coma one more time. Once again, her suffering made the front pages and the public held its breath.

When she came out of the clinic, she was too exhausted to return to Paris and Théo had to find somewhere new as a refuge in the same region. His choice was the little village of Plescassier, near Grasse, and a lovely villa, the ideal place for someone convalescing. He had decided to reduce their personnel: they only kept on Simone, the secretary, Danielle, the cook, Suzanne and the chauffeur, Christian. Visits were also kept to a minimum.

Théo said to me, 'You should go back to boulevard Lannes, Christie. We've talked about it with Loulou. It's best for there to be as few people as possible around Edith.'

Théo and Edith also wanted me to keep an eye on the apartment, especially with regard to journalists. I said goodbye to Francis, who was staying on the Côte d'Azur to make the most of his family for a bit longer. We promised to talk on the phone every day. With a heavy heart, I got on the train back to Paris, where, as in July, I knew that I would pass the majority of my time waiting for news.

At first, it wasn't too bad. Edith was a little better, Théo declared. She had phases of gaiety and optimism; she went out into the garden; she was even keen to play a game of boules sometimes. But, more and more frequently, these happy moments were followed by episodes which left her drained of all her strength. At these times, she would cry softly, looking at the garden as if watching life itself disappear or she would ask to listen to some records, and it felt like she was grieving for the loss of song itself – that *chanson* which had been her whole life.

Things followed their strange course until the end of September. Théo told me on the phone that Edith was 'stable', that she 'wasn't doing badly', but I sensed from his tone of voice that he was very anxious. Perhaps he was trying to convince himself that there were reasons to be optimistic.

'Do you want me to come down? Do you need me?'

I was ready to re-pack my suitcase and head off back to the south – besides, I couldn't concentrate on anything in Paris. But my question went unanswered and I could tell that my brother was distraught.

'When are you coming back?'

'Not straight away, Christie. Not yet. Perhaps we'll stay a month longer.'

I remember his telephone call of 10th October – one year and one day after their wedding. It was the end of the afternoon. Each time I heard the phone ring, it made me jump; unconsciously, I must have been waiting for the terrible announcement. I ran to get the phone. It was Théo. His voice was different and he told me, 'Christie, Edith is dead.'

It is always difficult to face the fact that someone we love has gone. The event seems unreal. The threads that link our existences are too numerous. The void that arrives with such violence is incomprehensible. Edith was also so much more for us than a loved one. She was an icon, she seemed immortal. And besides, for months now she'd been having crises and comas only to come through, renewed and ready to take on the fight again!

I sat down because my legs were betraying me; the pain was too strong I held the phone glued to my ear. 'You must be suffering so much, Théo…'

'It's terrible. I was there afterwards.'

'How did it happen?'

Edith had taken her last breath that same day, at the start of the afternoon, when Théo was on the road, driving back to her. She had a bad headache all of a sudden and, holding her head in her hands, said to Simone, 'What's happening to me?' Then, 'I need to go and lie down.'

The nurse accompanied her to her room. Edith stretched out on the bed. The next second, she was dead. A ruptured aneurysm. A vein had burst, caused by her liver disease.

Théo had found her dead.

'Christie, listen carefully.'

At the other end of the phone, I was crying.

'Are you listening?'

'Yes.'

'I don't want the news to get out yet. Nor for the whole world to turn up at Plascassier. I'm going to find an ambulance to transport her to boulevard Lannes. Paris needs to pay homage one last time.

Please don't say anything, Christie! It's really important!'

I kept the news to myself. I said nothing to anyone, not to my parents, not even to Francis. I stayed crying in the dark, near the phone, without moving, without doing anything. When the ringing started again, I would pick up the phone, then hang up straight away if it wasn't Théo at the end of the line. An hour later, I finally heard his voice.

'I found an ambulance, it's sorted. They've agreed to bring us back to Paris: Edith, Simone and I.'

It goes without saying that the ambulanceman had no idea that his patient was dead; he thought he was just transferring someone.

Théo continued, 'Whatever you do, don't pick up the phone from now on. We'll drive through the night. We'll be at boulevard Lannes at about five in the morning. You need to be ready for us then. When you see the ambulance arrive, open the garden door. But don't put any lights on in the library.

As it turned out, day had not yet dawned when I looked through the window and saw the ambulance being parked in silence in front of 67bis, boulevard Lannes. My brother got out of the vehicle. Simone too. I went to open up. I didn't switch on any lights. Théo took Edith in his arms and carried her as far as the apartment, then into their bedroom. The ambulance went away. The door closed once more.

A bit later, Danielle turned up. She'd helped Simone to jam Edith's jaw shut with a scarf. After that, a team of undertakers arrived to embalm the body. At the end of these distressing preparations, Edith was laid in a coffin, which had a small opening that allowed her face to be seen. She was carried like this into the library and exhibited on a high table.

For Théo and Loulou Barrier, the moment had now come to notify the press and the police. As was to be expected, the news spread like wildfire. One of the first people affected was Jean Cocteau, who was resting at home in Milly-La-Forêt. His own health was not good. He was suffering from pulmonary oedema. He'd had a heart attack in the spring and, from his bed, had written a letter to Edith containing the mysterious words, 'Rescued from the jaws of death I know not how (that's our thing)...' This 11th October, a few minutes after he learned that Edith was no more, he received a phone call from a journalist who asked him for his reaction and this comment is attributed to him, 'The ship stops sailing.' An hour later, he also died.

At boulevard Lannes, I no longer recognised the library which once provided the backdrop to my night-time conversations with Edith. The coffin on the table seemed like a monument. Thick ropes were ready. A red carpet was rolled out on the floor, leading outside to the little garden. The entrance to the building was protected by barriers intended to contain the crowd; they say more than three million fans came over several days to pay homage to Piaf, outside the building. The door of the apartment was only closed in the evening. We spent the whole day in the kitchen with Théo. He was suffering terribly. I tried to speak to him, to relieve his pain, to make him say something. I murmured banalities. 'Do you realise how many people are filing past? Everyone has come.'

'I knew they would. That's why I wanted to bring her back to Paris.'

'You don't want to go out for a bit? Go out and talk to them.'

'I don't want to steal Edith's show. They're here for her, not for me.'

But I could tell that some of them were there to console him, at least to offer him their condolences. However, he preferred to keep to himself. He stayed sitting in a chair, or in an armchair, to think about Edith, whom he'd lost. As he wasn't sleeping any more, he was exhausted. From time to time, his nerves gave way and he cried, which was shocking for me to see as I'd never seen my brother cry. While I was comforting him, strange memories of our previous life popped into my head, long conversations from the past in the hairdressing salon. When a client said to Papa, in a reproachful tone, 'You are too good to your children,' he would respond tranquilly, 'I want them to enjoy their happiness because we don't know what the future holds in store for them.' Now, I could appreciate the value of that reflection.

The funeral took place at Père-Lachaise Cemetery. It was impossible to forget an event like that first of all, before the body was collected, the music-hall stars cutting through the crowd to enter the library and bow in front of Edith's face, anonymous fans responding ardently to questions from reporters; then the undertakers in full uniform; the three, black funeral cars, piled high with mountains of flowers, leaving boulevard Lannes and crossing Paris; the entrance to Père-Lachaise taken over by forty thousand Parisians in mourning, who had been waiting since the early hours to see the cortège arrive; the police roadblocks worn down during the peak of the crowding; the silhouette of Marlene Dietrich moving sadly towards Edith's grave, where everyone wanted to be, and where an Orthodox priest was in charge; the journalists, perched on the surrounding tombstones; the walkways heaped with wreaths as no-one knew where to put them; Théo, as deeply wrapped in his black coat as in loneliness and grief.

He took his place with Loulou in the car which followed immediately behind the coffin. I was with my family in the next vehicle. The cortège, behind us, stretched out endlessly. Many people had taken a day's leave in order to attend the funeral. Each of us felt that the crowd was there to receive some comfort, not to enjoy a spectacle, because it was a piece of our own lives that was gone forever with Piaf. The ceremony at the cemetery was followed by a mass in front of the grave, in the course of which the priest quoted the 23rd Psalm:

> *The Lord is my shepherd; I shall not want.*
> *He maketh me to lie down in green pastures; he leadeth me beside the still waters.*
> *He restoreth my soul; he leadeth me in the paths of righteousness for his name's sake.*

I was not in any way religious at that time, but I felt that the verses helped me to endure the ordeal and to prepare me for tough months to come, through what they awoke in me.

20

A resonant voice woke me in the middle of the night – it was Edith's. I was sitting in my bed. I tried to gather my thoughts but I felt totally lost. That engaging voice, so familiar... where was it coming from? From another world? No, simply from the library. Edith wasn't singing, she was speaking. I couldn't quite understand what she was saying. But I was sure now that I wasn't dreaming. I got up and tip-toed along as far as the library, where the door was half-open. Théo was sitting there, in the shadows, wearing his dressing-gown, leaning over a tape-recorder that was on. He was listening to Edith's voice on a tape that he had recorded during one of their rehearsals. Edith was giving out advice, demonstrating by example, explaining nuances, suddenly going off at a tangent, bursting into laughter. I sat down in an arm-chair, without making any noise. I disciplined myself to be as quiet as possible. Not for anything would I have interrupted Théo's meditation. He carried on listening. After a while, I heard him murmur, 'It's as if she's still here.'

He seemed to be in full, spiritual communication with her. He added, turning towards me, 'Don't you think so?'

I just nodded for 'yes'; I had tears in my eyes. 'That's the impression I had when I woke up.'

Théo continued to listen to his recording. He replayed the tape over and over. From time to time, he glanced in my direction. Seeing that my eyes were red, he said to me, 'You must be tired. Go back to bed, Christie.'

'And you, aren't you tired?'

He too had tears in his eyes. 'I'm going to stop. I'm going to try to sleep. Thank you for keeping me company.'

This sort of thing happened often. It was Théo's way of controlling his grief; still spending time with Edith, listening to her talk, filling the void with her voice.

During this period, Théo refused to go out and see people. Nothing appealed to him. As he couldn't get to sleep at night, he ended up taking sleeping tablets. He then spent a good part of each day in bed. Friends called, inviting him out for a drink, for a change of scenery, but he didn't feel up to seeing anyone. The fact was that I was his only company. Théo had watched over me all my childhood and ever since I'd left La Frette. It was my turn, now, to protect him, to help him get through this difficult time, to live in this big apartment. Suzanne and Christiane, the cooks, had gone. Théo no longer had the means to pay them. However, he had kept on Danielle, the secretary, and Christian, the chauffeur. Simone, the nurse, sometimes visited us for friendship's sake.

A maid came each day to take care of the house, run errands, cook a little. I did my best to give her useful instructions. Or, to be more precise, to pass on those my brother gave. He banned me from doing housework. According to him, I should instead continue to work, to write songs, to make records, as Edith had wished before passing on. It's true that I wanted to move up in the profession, but I felt too responsible for Théo to be able to concentrate on anything else.

Then, financial problems started to accumulate. Bills from doctors and clinics arrived, along with overdue tax demands. This was nothing new; money was in short supply even before Edith died. But Théo had stuck to his plan of renting the properties in the Midi, to ensure that she lacked for nothing. And so the debts were back. Now it was up to the tax authorities to recoup back payments for the year, which meant cutting Théo's means of living. I was very upset when I realised that he was forced to sell the collection of books he loved so much to antique dealers. He also gave up various objects, carpets – only those goods that belonged to him personally – not touching Edith's. Now and then our parents helped us. They would come to boulevard Lannes with money, a roast chicken, other meat, fruit. Whatever the situation, they never turned up empty-handed. And they didn't ask too many questions. These problems had their positive side because they proved yet again the strength of the links uniting our family.

One day when he came into my room, Papa saw that I had pinned on the wall a photo of the Lamboukas children, all together: Théo, my sister and I. He had this to say: 'I have a priceless treasure, and here it is.' Then he added, 'And I have another one, in my wife.'

I have never forgotten this declaration of love; even today, it's as if Papa made this statement only five minutes ago.

The months which followed the loss of Edith seemed an eternity to me. At night, I would hear my brother pacing up and down the apartment; his steps echoed in the hallway, in the big lounge, and ended up in the library, where he would press buttons on the tape recorder to listen again to the tapes, over and over. The next day, he would sleep almost the whole day. So I suggested that he take a walk along the woodland paths.

'You think I should?' he said. He didn't want to.

I insisted: 'You can't stay cooped up all the time. It's a lovely day. Don't you want to make the most of the sunshine?'

'I don't care,' he sighed. Finally, he agreed to come with me for a short walk. I was sure that he was doing it for my sake, knowing how much I suffered from seeing him so depressed. He was still trying to protect me. Soon we were walking along the paths, in the dappled light filtered through leaves. These walks were always in silence, as Théo said nothing; he pursued his own train of thought. When we paused to look at the lake, I wondered whether he could really see it. I tried to bring him back to present-day reality.

'It's beautiful isn't it, the view?'

'Yes, it's pretty.'

Walkers, children, boy scouts passing by, people in rowboats or dinghies; nothing piqued his curiosity. From time to time, we would climb into the ferryman's boat. We would then get off on the other bank, where a tea-room offered strawberry tarts taken out of the oven that very day. The tea was delicious. Théo began to relax. And even if he'd made the effort to come out with the sole aim of keeping me happy, I knew that this recreation was good for him too.

Then, as the months went by, I saw his morale gradually improve. He accepted the contract offered to him by Loulou Barrier for a series of concerts in Belgium. Théo remembered travelling across that country with Edith and how happy they'd been there. This was how the public started to get used to seeing Théo alone on stage. Wherever he gave concerts, he was well received. Of course, through him, the public could still think about Piaf, of the souvenir she'd left in their hearts. But, from that time on, the papers presented Théo Sarapo as a singer and an actor, with no other references. On his return from Belgium, he had recovered some of his self-assurance, and even high spirits. Friends called on boulevard Lannes and encouraged him to move on.

They told him, 'Follow Edith's example. She always wanted to move forward, you know that. She wouldn't like you to throw in the towel.'

Among the visitors was Charles Aznavour, who said to me, teasing, 'So, what's this I hear, that you've been sleeping in my bedroom?'

That's where he had lived, when he started out, at the time when Edith had taught him his profession.

'What was it like?' I asked him.

'She would never let anything go, believe me. If something wasn't quite right, I had to keep going back to it.'

To be with him, right by the piano, in the main lounge, where Edith's presence still lingered, was like passing time with the family, chatting happily. Other singers also came to help Théo, in memory of Edith, and because they felt sympathy for him.

After my insistence, and that of his friends, Théo decided that he had to start going out. But on one occasion, when he'd dined out and had drunk a glass or two, someone pushed a girl into his arms at the end of the evening, as if it were a game. On the spot, a reporter took a photo of the scene. It was a set-up by the journalists. The image appeared in the press with the caption, *Edith dead, Théo Sarapo celebrates.* My brother was very depressed by this incident, knowing that he was under the media's scrutiny, from now on and that he would be criticised however he behaved. He continued to go out. He even spent time with women who were interested in him. These liaisons never lasted though. In all these new faces, it was Edith's that he sought, and, because of that, these 'love affairs' soon died.

The entertainment world wanted to express its affection and solidarity. Many of those who had been friends of the Piaf-Sarapo couple pulled out all the stops to support Théo, especially as his financial problems were known to everyone. Certain journalists also made every effort to keep his head above water. That was how Loulou Barrier was able to organise galas and tours throughout Europe with Théo Sarapo as the star. On other occasions he shared the billing with a famous artist, such as Enrico Macias, who was very considerate towards us. I could also cite Annie Cordy, Alice Dona, Salvatore Adamo, not only colleagues but genuine friends, with whom he was lucky enough to get on really well. Dalida also helped him. I had seen her many times at boulevard Lannes during Edith's life and Edith was very fond of her. Dalida even treated me, who wasn't famous, in a friendly manner. Maintaining her affection for Théo was a way to stay faithful to Piaf, and Théo appreciated that. Piaf and Dalida had the same conception of the artist's profession to be disciplined, to bring your work back to the workshop twenty times and polish it to pursue without respite the goal of inaccessible perfection. Many great names, famous to the media, contributed through their friendship to Théo's success in the years which followed Edith's death. That was the case with Philippe Bouvard, who often mentioned Théo during his broadcasts, and with Michel Drucker. This support proved to be useful in overcoming the sort of petty jealousy that could be found in the small world of Parisian variety shows. Théo took six months to propel himself to the forefront of the scene, an ascent so rapid that it inevitably aroused spiteful gossip. Yet envious comments didn't damage the public's esteem for him. Théo had showed without a doubt that he loved his wife truly, deeply. Those who often came to boulevard Lannes in Edith's lifetime could only confirm that.

A gala that counted for a great deal during this difficult period when Théo was obliged to start over was organised in Greece. I accompanied him on the voyage, and I remember how happy I was to see him smiling again, appreciating life. It was the time when *Zorba the Greek* was a hit on the big screen, with Anthony Quinn in the truculent, wild, leading role. In Paris, Théo had caused a sensation by dancing the sirtaki, Zorba's dance, at the Saint-Hilaire Club. He started it again in Athens, at a restaurant where we were invited to dine after his performance. In Greece, everyone opened their arms out wide to him. Théo had arrived glowing with the aura of his origins, of his amazing destiny, and of course with his artistic talent. I remember clearly that extraordinary evening when I saw my brother become himself once more. People were breaking plates – a much-prized from of entertainment in Athens at the time. The whole room was dancing, hands on each other's shoulders. The party lasted until Homer's 'rosy-fingered dawn' tinted the sky behind the olive trees. Then, the friend who'd invited us took us into the countryside for breakfast, to the house of a woman he knew. This lady served us bread fresh from the oven, with honey and feta cheese. There was tea and Greek coffee. We were exhausted, but so happy to do our hostess proud! For my part, I was brimming with happiness; Théo had come to experience his renaissance in the land of his ancestors. I felt completely serene when I was taken back to the hotel. But not Théo; he didn't want to go back, nor to rest. He preferred to stay outside, to savour the glorious light. And he set off to swim in the sea with a small gang of companions. Once more in Paris, seeing as Théo was better, I had enough leisure time to think about my career as a singer. It had been interrupted by Edith's death, even though it had been close to her heart and she'd encouraged me to work, and then work some more, to always go further. It was she who'd pushed me to go on stage, to perfect my voice. Music had come into my life well before I was an adult. My parents sat me at the piano from a very young age, and I won my first prize during a contest for which Papa had registered me, at Salle Gaveau. Of course, these last few months, I'd tended to follow in my brother's footsteps, given that he'd always done everything he could to advise me and encourage my efforts. Now that life was renewing its demands, I started rehearsing again. I worked with Théo and with Noël Commaret, who had started composing for me, while continuing to play the piano for my brother during concerts.

I was no longer going out with Francis. Our relationship had lasted a year. I had felt secure in the arms of this sweet-natured, considerate young man. We'd had marvellous moments together on the Côte d'Azur; we'd been inseparable, everyone treated us protectively, with affection. And I could not forget the simple warmth of the welcome given to me by his parents in Nice. However, I was young, I was still growing up, in my heart, in my head. Now I needed to breathe, to feel I was truly my own person. Our love affair came to an end naturally, without shouting, tears or drama. Besides, Francis, ever the workaholic, was going to be very busy in the years following Edith's death. He composed the film score for *A man and a woman* – the lyrics were written by Pierre Barough. Then, building on that success, he wrote the music for *Love Story*. His career was already prestigious when we were going for a spin, hair flying in the wind, in the Nice hinterland. With what followed, it would become a triumph. As a companion, he left me with marvellous memories.

I not only liked singing, but also writing songs, such as *Agatha or Christie?*, which was often on the air at the end of the sixties. My compositions had that lightness of tone that was the hallmark of variety at that time, and differed hugely from the style of Edith Piaf! Her world kept going a popular tradition that dated back to the nineteenth century; her songs told whole stories, sometimes melodramatic, although she herself had a great sense of humour. While she was alive, I was in awe of Edith, as a singer and as a woman, but I never imagined becoming 'like her', either on a professional level or as a human being. The influence she'd exercised over me had been moral. She did everything to awaken my self-determination.

And now that she wasn't there any more, I often remembered a long conversation that we'd had in her blue-papered dressing-room, one evening when she was putting on her make-up and when she sensed that I was discouraged.

'Listen to me, Christie, I know you love singing. You love music, the cinema. You love the arts in general. You can work your way up, show what you can do. That's what I did!'

I was distraught at seeing her worried to such a degree over me. I replied timidly, 'I don't have your voice, Edith. Or your talent.'

'That seems out of reach to you?'

'Yes. You rose so high. I will never get there.'

'You're wrong! You can do it! You have your own personality. And a passion. That's what you have to nurture.' She was insistent, showing all the passion necessary, 'Don't let yourself be discouraged. Keep at it.'

I felt that what she was trying to pass on to me was her own courage.

'There will always be people who try and put you down. Don't listen to them. Continue to make progress. Look straight ahead of you. You think they didn't criticise me? They even tried to destroy me, can you imagine? But I kept at it. And so, here I am.'

'I kept at it, here I am'; she had a powerful way of saying those words, she put her whole heart into them, as she did when on stage. She added, 'When I go under, I let myself sink. I slip right to the bottom. That lasts two days! After that, I give myself a good kicking and rise to the surface again. When I'm back to normal, I hit the ground running. I'm unstoppable.'

This exchange, which lasted at least two hours, left me exhausted and at the same time buoyant with hope. Edith was blessed with powers of persuasion that nothing could shake.

'You have so many qualities, Christie. So many qualities which haven't fully awoken yet. They will be revealed one day.'

Then she showed that benevolent smile that was hers alone. 'I get the impression that you've been listening to me. I can see it in your eyes.'

I said nothing. I watched her smile and read my mind.

'Come on, let's go. Let's take a turn. Afterwards, we can come back and have a cup of tea.'

Nowadays, each time the memory of Edith's encouragement comes back to me, I'm reminded of a quotation from St Paul,

I can do all things through Him who strengthens me

Influenced by the encouragement that Edith had lavished on me when she was alive, I tried to find my own way and my own voice. That's how I made the lesson part of my life. If I intended to imitate Edith, it would be through the act of exercising my will, not through the manner in which I did so.

I had adopted the habit of drawing inspiration from the carefree paths in the Bois de Boulogne rather than from scouring the 'miscellaneous' sections in newspapers. I would wander there every day in the company of a cocker spaniel someone had given me as a present. According to his pedigree, he was named Richard de Lagrange, but I'd renamed him Zouzou. Once again, I'd chosen something light-hearted, fun; Théo even found this name a bit ridiculous, when he heard me calling it. However that may be, these walks inspired me with ideas for amusing songs.

Jacques Poisson, Théo's artistic director at Pathé Marconi, decided that I should definitely sign a recording contract with him. That was how I came to join this record label after my first two forty-fives at Barclay's. I recorded numbers like *Rouge rouge*, *L'Adorable Femme des neiges*, and also *La Musique et la Danse*. *Agatha ou Christie* too, the track I've already mentioned. Loulou Barrier stayed as my manager. He made me take part in television commercials, or enter competitions, such as *La Rose de France*, which took place in Antibes.

Thanks to all of this, I was lucky enough to get to know Michèle Arnaud, the ex-singer, author and television producer, really well. Michèle had launched Serge Gainsbourg, whom she loved. I was far from having Gainsbourg's talent, but she liked me too, as an artist, and she tried to promote me. One day, when Théo and I were at Bernard Dimey's, we met Serge Gainsbourg, the man himself. He had not yet developed the 'Gainsbarre' style. He didn't say much, but you could tell that he already had the art of encapsulating the music of his time. He wrote a song for me that I recorded for Pathé Marconi, sadly lost today. With Michèle, I went on a trip to Warsaw, where we took in that strange, disturbing atmosphere that was the cold war. I felt completely part of the yé-yé movement which held sway during the sixties. It was the era of Richard Anthony – with whom I cut the duet *Comment tu fais?* on the disc *Le Grand Meaulnes* – and of Sheila the era of mini-skirts and forty-five records, which the teenagers played on their Teppaz decks at their rave-ups so they could dance and make contact with the opposite sex.

Springtime of 1967 stays in my memory as perhaps the most romantic episode of my life. Théo was doing much better at this point. He worked a lot and so did I. We were still staying at the apartment on boulevard Lannes and sometimes, when we felt the need to relax, we would invite friends round. They would appear with other friends, and so on, as is almost always how it works. At one of these evenings, G turned up, a man I'd never seen before, and who made a very strong impression on me at first sight. Obviously, one reason I was so interested in him was that he glanced my way all the time, still talking all the while within his little group. G was good-looking, elegant, attractive. Our eyes met again and again. However, when he detached himself from his little gang to come and engage me in conversation, suggesting that we should go out together one evening, my immediate response was, 'No'. I said 'No,' but my whole being was shouting an enthusiastic 'Yes!' But G attracted me too much. I was shocked by the depth of feeling that he'd already aroused in me, when we'd barely exchanged three words – as someone can be terrified on the brink of a strange country that is open to his intrepid discovery, so rich but also full of those dangers known as grief and disappointment. I had made some progress since Edith had pushed me into Francis' arms. I was no longer the naive little girl fallen from the family nest.

I was beginning to have some idea of what love was – that battlefield between joy and pain. And I could still hear, ringing in my ears, the words Edith had spoken in the old days, in the shadows of the library, 'You'll know it's true love when you find it'. However that might be, G reappeared after a few days. I must confess that I thought of him each time the phone rang, echoing throughout the apartment. However, when I did recognise his voice at the end of the line, it was as if I was once more turned to stone. To the point where I don't even remember any more what he suggested that day: dinner, a film, a drink at the Saint-Hilaire, it doesn't matter. A few more days went by, then he called yet again. It was one evening at five o'clock. I had just come home to boulevard Lannes after spending the afternoon in the Porte Dauphine swimming pool. The telephone rang. G offered to come and pick me up in his car. This was his third attempt. I had nothing else planned... I said 'O.K.' like someone diving into the abyss. Then I hung up and went to pretty myself.

G took me to dine at the Eiffel Tower. And as the atmosphere was very warm, we went for a walk along the quayside. After the quay, we went on to a club. We danced. We drank Jack and coke cocktails – the height of fashion at the time. Towards four o'clock in the morning, G asked me if I liked bowling. I had never even set foot in a bowling alley! This was a big learning curve for me. G was not only considerate, but took care to very closely follow my progress in every way. When we had left the bowling alley, he took me in his arms, which had the consequence of depriving me of all reason. And I don't think he was far from going to pieces as well.

We went out together all that year. G was a student in a business school. He came from a well-off family. As for me, however tentatively, I was pursuing a career as a singer, which Jacques Poisson, my artistic director, considered to be slow in getting off the ground. But nothing really upset us, G and me. We found enough to enchant us in our endless conversations and in feeling good together. Théo had accepted my boyfriend and decided to leave us in peace, so G came every day to boulevard Lannes. Sometimes, he simply stayed there with me. On other evenings, we would go to the Saint-Hilaire, meet up with some friends and have a ball. The relationship was carefree and rich at the same time. There were no undercurrents between us. We rejoiced in our freedom, in a Paris where the winds of liberty were whirling through the streets. And we felt that we were made to be together; in essence, our meeting could well have led to marriage, a true love-match.

But destiny decided otherwise. A previous liaison caught up with G, who had to leave me to marry another woman, against his will.

21

Even though I had a record about to come out, my career as a singer seemed to be in freefall. At least, that was Jacques Poisson's opinion. Rather brusquely, he advised me to take a detour via films.

'While you're waiting for things to start up again,' he told me. 'You can make two or three films, then get back into the music world.'

This would have been possible. For example, since filming *Judex*, Théo had made friends in the seventh art. He had then got a role in *Un condé*, by Yves Boisset. The problem was that I wasn't at all sure that I wanted to follow him into acting. The prospect of playing a part in front of a camera applealed to me, but no more than that. In fact, the milieu itself frightened me a little. I far preferred the company of music-hall artists, who formed a permanent relationship with their public. On the other hand, it was important to move with the times, as Edith would have said. In reality, I was going through a period of great confusion, no doubt indicative of my internal upheaval. The split with G had left me feeling annihilated. I found myself at a dead end in every respect. I had lost my sense of direction. I needed to concentrate so I could reflect on all that had happened to me. One day, when I confided my worries to Simone, Edith's ex-nurse, she put an idea to me.

'You know there are jobs going in Greece?'

'What sort of jobs, exactly, Simone?

'Tourist guides.'

Greece appealed to me and awoke in me many emotions, not only because of its incredible beauty, but also because it was where my ancestors had first seen the light of day. Since my first trip out there with Maman, I loved to contemplate the sky that their eyes had seen. I thought that, sometimes, a journey helps someone to forget their sorrows – or at least allows them to leave them behind for a little while. I sent a letter of application to the Airtour Agency, not forgetting to mention that I spoke French, Greek and English. A week later, I was taking tourists to visit the Acropolis or Delphi. My work consisted of taking charge of groups when they left Paris and acting as their guide throughout their stay in Greece. For ten days, the holiday-makers were booked into a village situated by the seaside, between Athens and Corinth: Kalogria. Bungalows had been built in this paradise, along with a restaurant supplied by local fishermen. Every ten days, I accompanied my group back to the airport and returned to Kalogria with the next one, freshly arrived from Paris.

Not far from Kalogria was Tanagra, the site of the American military base where personnel from the U.S. Air Force were stationed. Three times a week, pilots came to Kalogria to bathe, to have a drink, to make the most of the restaurant, to relax on the beach. These airmen were welcomed as friends by the Greeks, as were the French tourists who had come to luxuriate in the sun. Perhaps I needed to forget my disappointment with G, perhaps my life was seeking a new direction... In any case, something started up with an airman whose nickname to his friends was 'Chis'. He and his gang made regular visits to the restaurant and Chis's eyes often met mine. I had a lot of time on my hands; the role of tour guide was not too demanding. And everything contributed to the creation of an idyll: the atmosphere of summer freedom, the infinite blue of the sea, those heavenly landscapes straight from legend. Our relationship was born the day Chis decided to detach himself from his group of five friends for five minutes so that he could come over at last and introduce himself. He started a conversation with me in a manner that was simple, direct, very much in the American style. It was like pushing open the door to another world.

At first, Chis seemed to be looking only for friendship. Perhaps he was still a bit shy. Or maybe it was my life that intrigued him, with its slightly picturesque aspect; he had found a French girl of Greek origin who'd made records in Paris. For my part, I wanted to get to know this man who was so kind, considerate and patient better. The Kalogria restaurant featured an orchestra each night. Chis and I always sat at the same table, in front of the sea, which changed colour as the sun set. Chis helped me make progress in American English, which is so different from the British language. We had long conversations, during which each of us opened our heart, a bit at a time, and the link between us grew stronger. Chis, who'd lost his father when he was nine, really wanted to have a wife, children, a family to love. I could tell that we were always on the same wavelength when this subject came up. Me too, I wanted to start a family. Not to put right any cruel void, as was the case with him, but because I'd lived in a united and happy household, and I hoped to reproduce these feelings. So, in essence, our exchanges were concerned with the future, something that was new for me. With Francis, and the same with G, the relationship was always nurtured by the present; we wanted to make the most of life, rather than construct plans. Suddenly, everything was different. I'd changed, and Chis was the incarnation of that change. Each evening in that period, I waited impatiently for his visit. When he couldn't get away from the base, he would send me a tender note that I would read several times before pressing it against my heart.

In September, when I returned to Paris, after spending two months in Greece, I was no longer the same person. I couldn't see where I fitted in. All my thoughts were of Kalogria and I missed Chis. He missed me too, obviously.

'Come back, Christie,' he said on the phone.

Almost straight away, I jumped on a plane to go back and throw myself into his arms. By October, I was expecting a baby. We decided to get married in Athens, or, more precisely, at Pangrati, the quarter where some of my family lived. The wedding would take place according to Orthodox rites. Unfortunately, neither my parents nor Théo were able to come.

My parents had money problems, caused by helping Théo pay off his debts. And as for Théo, he was on tour. But on my side that day I had Maman's sister, her husband (my uncle) and, of course, my cousins. My sister, who'd married a Greek, was among the group. The religious ceremony ran on into a celebration: dinner in a restaurant where Dalaras was performing, a singer already popular at that time. Our honeymoon, the next day, was mainly spent obtaining our marriage certificates to pass them on to the American military hierarchy and the French authorities.

The family we'd dreamed of was about to be born. In April we would leave for the United States; ten hours on a plane to reach New York, then three hours to get to Atlanta, and another hour and a half to Tampa in Florida. In fact, the Chilsholms had settled in Winter Heaven, east of Tampa and its bay. Chis's mother welcomed me with open arms, very affectionately. Everyone was looking forward to the happy occasion. The garden was full of grapefruit trees laden with fruit. I was in heaven. Without even knowing it, I had been hoping for this uprooting, a change of scenery. Chis, delighted at finding his native country again, brought me hamburgers, 'French fries' and strawberry milkshakes. We grew excited over plans for the child. The intense heat made my pregnancy complicated but without dampening my optimism.

My husband decided to buy a car, and we headed off west, to Alamagordo, the military base in New Mexico to which Chis was now assigned. During a stop at New Orleans, we took a room in the French

Quarter. I still remember our dinner in the hotel restaurant: the lace, table-linen, old-fashioned silver cutlery, the waiter in white gloves. The décor of *Gone with the Wind*! After dinner, we went for a walk through the streets, where jazz songs and Cajun music wafted out from all directions. The next stage of the journey took us to Mississippi, Alabama, Texas. At San Antonio, the hotel decor became unequivocally Mexican. The long freeway of El Paso was deserted. The desert stretched out on both sides, dotted with shrubs that had been dried out by the sun and wind. The silhouettes of solitary hills were outlined against a sky of almost metallic blue, the opposite of Greek skies. And suddenly an isolated house appeared – a restaurant.

The owner, a charming little woman, welcomed us to a table, tying on her apron. This endless road had woken a kind of sadness in me; I had the feeling that I was going further than ever away from my parents and my brother. We were served with iced tea in big glasses, then a casserole which reminded me of bœuf bourguignon, with fresh bread, strawberry tart and rhubarb. I took care to thank the owner for the excellent meal. But, still feeling weighed down, I couldn't help asking, 'Aren't you afraid?'

'Afraid of what?'

'Of living like this, all alone in the desert.'

'I'm not alone. I have passers-by every day. Anyone who goes from El Paso to San Antonio stops at my place. Whether for lunch or whether to deliver something.'

'But in the evenings, you're alone.'

'I'm used to that.'

The fate of this woman tormented me. How could someone live in such isolation? Chis took my hand and gently reassured me.

The next day we reached El Paso. At last. I was exhausted. I went straight upstairs to our bedroom to lie down. Then I fell asleep.

It was five in the morning when the pains started. My waters had broken. Chis ran into the bathroom to fetch a big absorbent towel that he put on me like a nappy, closing it with safety pins as if he were my nanny. I slipped on my housecoat. The next minute we were driving through the night. Chis was hitting the accelerator hard. A police officer gave chase. He ordered us to pull over.

'My wife is about to give birth!' Chis shouted at him through the open window.

'Follow me.'

Sirens blaring, he opened the route for us right to the military hospital.

I ended up in a U.S. Army medical centre, a series of wooden barracks where they played the bugle at dawn and dusk. It was in these strange surroundings that labour commenced; thirty-six painful hours which ended in a Caesarean, followed by an infection. I came round from the anaesthetic only to fall into a nightmare; they had carried me to a double room, and the next bed was occupied by a patient about fifty years old, with a device fitted in his skull. But the nightmare changed to a fairy-tale when the nurse presented my son to me – born in El Paso, on the border of New Mexico.

Ten months later, after our return to Florida, our second child arrived, a little girl, born in Pensacola.

At Alamagordo, as there was no house available in the area defined as the military zone, the command lodged us in one of a dozen trailers located in the middle of the desert, all occupied by soldiers' families. It was summer once again. Chis and I had known each other for a year. We'd been married nine months. Our son had only been in existence for a few weeks. There were numerous difficulties but we were happy.

22

At Alamagordo, work was taking up all of Chis's attention and I had a lot of time for reflection when the baby was sleeping or babbling peacefully while playing with his rattle in his cradle. Inevitably, my thoughts took me to France, to Paris, to memories of La Frette, to my parents, to Edith and Théo. When I'd set off for Greece so I could go back to Chis – and marry him – I'd had the vague feeling that I was abandoning my brother and his fate. I had watched over him a great deal after Edith's death, when he'd had so much difficulty in getting over his grief, in recovering a taste for life. Then he started to come out of it. He'd taken up with friends again, renewed his old ways at Saint-Hilaire. He even had a few love affairs. But you could always sense a kind of melancholy in him. His moody charm, that sombre beauty which he seemed to radiate, all expressed this feeling. I remember a discussion that we had at boulevard Lannes, one evening when he seemed depressed.

'Didn't Loulou suggest tours in Mexico and Canada for you?'

'Yes. But I told him no.'

'Travelling would do you good. And you need to expand your audience. Why did you turn it down?'

He had this strange reaction: 'Because I was too afraid of dying far away from Maman and Papa.'

He was only thirty-three years old and he was musing on death. Did he have a dark premonition? Did he guess that his destiny would be tragic? I knew that he was consulting André Barbeau – Edith's astrologer, whom they were in the habit of seeing together. Had Barbeau said something to Théo? There was some mystery in all this. Théo knew, and I knew too that a clairvoyant had once made such a terrifying prediction to Maman that she could never dismiss it from her thoughts. 'One of your children will die young.' At Alamagordo, my thoughts often returned to my brother, to what he'd said in a worried tone when I'd set off for Greece. 'Hurry back.'

I did in fact go back. In the September. But I did so only to leave almost straight away. And Théo had not been able to attend my wedding, which had upset him a lot. From the United States, I'd written to him to announce the birth of my son – also to tell him about the interminable labour, and of the trailer that served as our home in the middle of the desert. He had replied to this letter with another one, in which he expressed his concern. 'Are you sure you're happy? You're not hiding something from me?' I wasn't hiding anything from him. I was happy, despite everything. Because I had a husband, a child, plans for the family. In this letter, Théo let me know that he'd left boulevard Lannes to set up home in a smaller, cheaper apartment.

At the end of August in 1970, when my son was coming up to four months old, I received a phone call at Alamogordo. At first, I had difficulty recognising the person speaking to me. Then I realised that it was Théo's godmother. How was this even possible? She hardly ever called me! Before I heard a word of what she had to say, I knew something serious had happened. I exchanged looks with Chis, who had come to the same conclusion, and he pulled up a chair for me so I could sit down. I thought of Yaya, my grandmother, aged eighty-six. And, obviously, of my parents. But not for one moment did I think of Théo or my sister; they were too young to disappear.

From the other end of the line, Théo's godmother told me, 'Call your parents, Christie.'

'Can't you tell me anything?'

'I don't want to be the one who tells you the news...'

'But I want to know!'

I looked at my husband, terrified.

'Someone is dead...'

'Who?'

'Théo. A car accident.'

'You're sure? Perhaps he's just hurt?'

Théo was giving a series of concerts in France. As he didn't drive, it was Christian, the chauffeur, who was responsible for taking him from one concert to the next, no longer in Edith's legendary white Mercedes but in a recently acquired blue DS19. And, as this was during the school holidays, Christian had his ten-year old son next to him. Théo, Christian and the child stopped at Limoges to dine and spend the night. During the evening, my brother and the hotel owners became very friendly. This couple had two sons who played with Christian's boy. The parents were looking for a driver to take their boys somewhere the next day.

'We'll drop them off,' Théo offered.

The next morning, everyone set off in the car: Christian at the wheel, Théo in the passenger seat and the three boys in the back. Coming out of Panazol, at the spot called Château de la rue, a car coming in the opposite direction, driven recklessly, forced Christian to swerve violently, and the DS was smashed against a tree. Théo was flung forward and pierced by several shards of metal. When they arrived, the emergency services freed him, then took him to Limoges Hospital, where he died after three hours spent in agony. Christian, wounded in the stomach, came through it. The three boys, although very shocked, were unharmed.

I didn't get these details from the godmother, but from my parents shortly afterwards. When I phoned them, I had the crazy hope that they would tell me the horrible news was false. 'Perhaps this woman made it all up,' I kept telling myself. But Papa could only repeat what I'd just heard.

'Christie, Théo is dead.'

'And you didn't tell me! Put Maman on!'

'She's gone to lie down.'

A silence followed, then Maman's voice reached me, from way across the ocean.

'We were going to let you know, Christie. But not straight away, so as to not complicate your life, you're so far away…'

'When is the funeral?'

'Tomorrow.'

A mass had already been planned, as well as the burial at Père-Lachaise beside Edith. I had twenty-four hours in front of me. And I didn't want to go without my son. Unfortunately, he had no passport and not even a proper, official birth certificate. Since our wedding, everything had happened so quickly that we hadn't had time to get our papers in order. Chis mobilised the military base so we could have certificates immediately. An officer called the TWA company and made an arrangement so I could travel with my son of four-and-a-half months. It was agreed that my papers would be put in order during the connection to New York. Chis took us by car to El Paso. Then at John F. Kennedy airport, a police officer with special authority was waiting for us, holding a passport in my son's name and a provisional birth certificate. All that remained was for us to rush off to catch the 747 to Paris.

When we arrived at Orly, we had very little time to spare. My baby in my arms, I ran to get a taxi. Settling with difficulty into the car, I launched straight into instructions. 'Take me quickly to rue Georges-Bizet. The Orthodox Church. The funeral mass for my brother has already begun.'

'I know,' replied the taxi-driver, turning towards us. 'They announced it on the radio. Théo Sarapo's your brother, right?'

At rue Georges-Bizet the crowd had brought traffic to a standstill. I carved a route as far as the entrance to the church, which was of course swarming with people. The candles were flickering at the foot of the icons. Acquaintances turned their heads as I passed them. Some came to speak to me. At that moment, my strength left me; I had to entrust my son to a friend or I would never have been capable of walking up the nave. I could see, in the front pew, the sad faces of Papa, Maman, my sister – they were veiled in black. The priest was praying next to a coffin covered in flowers. I seized Maman's hands and she cried out, so loudly that the pries couldn't be heard, 'It's my daughter, Christie! Théo's sister. She's here from New Mexico! She's come here from the desert!'

I had no veil to cover my face. I was dressed in a lightweight black T-shirt and a simple black-and-white skirt. No doubt Maman's intention was to answer any questions people might be asking, even if no-one dared express them, to ensure the ceremony ran smoothly, without interruption. After these words, she said no more, leaving the floor to the priest once again. She was crying. She squeezed my hand between frozen fingers. Papa kissed me. His eyes were red. He said Maman wasn't up to coming to Père-Lachaise.

'Stay with her, I'll go with your sister.'

My friends handed my son back to me. The priest made us leave by a back door and I went to sit for a long while with Maman behind the church. She watched me rocking my baby. She was in despair. For a moment, she seemed lost in confusion, incapable of deciding whether she should cry over her son's death or rejoice at this almost miraculous apparition: her grandson's face.

Outside, ten thousand people accompanied Théo Sarapo to his last resting-place.

I didn't go back to the United States straight away. I spent a fortnight at La Frette. How strange my childhood town seemed now! So much had happened and so quickly! Was I still the same old Christie? At first, a flood of visitors arrived at my parents' door. Then it was reduced to a trickle. I talked a lot to Papa and Maman. I consoled them. I told them about our life in New Mexico. Despite their grief, they had the satisfaction of seeing a new-born baby present in their house. They could also see that I was happy; Chis called me every day on the phone.

'How did you find out about Théo's death?' I asked them one evening.

It was Papa who told me: 'We'd finished lunch and I was watching the television news. Only giving it half my attention. I was hearing it without listening, like we usually do. Then I sat up because Théo's name had been mentioned. The presenter was talking about Théo Sarapo. I called out to Maman, who was washing the dishes. She came through, wiping her hands, just at the moment they said that Théo was dead...'

Sobs broke up his words. 'They talked about a traffic accident near Limoges. They showed pictures of a DS completely wrecked. They said the driver had come out of it all right, and so had the three children who were in the back. But Théo died in hospital...'

'Papa! Don't tell me that no-one informed you! Did you really find out the news by watching television?'

'Yes, Christie. That's exactly how it happened. The hospital told us nothing. Nor did the journalists. It reached us via the television.'

Papa said nothing for a few seconds, then he added, 'When she heard that, Maman fainted.'

The next day, he decided not to let me know until after the funeral. I lived so far from Paris, I'd recently been through a very difficult labour, my child was still a baby: better to spare me the worry of a long journey. But Théo's godmother had let the cat out of the bag and everything had turned out differently. At the end of my stay, when I was about to leave La Frette to return home, Papa and Maman thanked me.

'It was good that you came.'

I returned to Alamagordo with my son. For several weeks, Chis said that I would startle him in the middle of the night by calling out my brother's name in my sleep.

I remember one particular day, when the wind was blowing a gale so strong that the sand stuck to the trailer windows. My husband was at the base. My son was sleeping in the next room. I was sitting on the bed. A thousand questions plagued me. Why do we exist? Why do we have to die? Why die at thirty-four years old? Why are some lives so short and others so long? What is truly important? I had known pride in reaching the top of the ladder, I had stayed in the suites of the most prestigious hotels and frequented the best restaurants in Europe. I had belonged to a refined, sophisticated, cultured society. I had been the friend and confidante of one of the greatest singers in history. Yet even so, my quest was not over. I wanted to continue the search. I wanted to end up with something better, something stronger, as powerful as love. I dropped to my knees, knowing what I was going to ask for. I closed my eyes and said the words softly.

'Lord Jesus, I give you my life, I let my self go into You.'

At that moment, I sensed the power of God, while the words of John the Evangelist came mysteriously to mind:

> *For God so loved the world, that he gave his only begotten Son, that whosoever believeth in him should not perish, but have everlasting life.*
> *For God sent not his Son into the world to condemn the world; but that the world through him might be saved.*

Ever since then, these words have stayed with me. And God Himself has never left me.

Epilogue

And so the story comes to an end...

An end? Everyone knows that the ending of one story is always the beginning of another. Perhaps I'll pick up a pen once more to recount in a new tale what became of me in America – the country in which I first set foot at twenty-eight years old, where I constructed a life and where I eventually wrote these pages.

I wanted to tell the story of how three lives were inter-connected: that of Piaf, Théo and my own life. I grew into adulthood at the same time as Edith experienced the ending of her life. Anyone who is dying looks back at the past, and for her I was the incarnation of that youthfulness she had loved so much. In the same way, everyone needs a guide as they pass from sullen adolescence into adulthood, and Edith was mine – she was even the one who created my stage name, as she had also done for Théo. It was Théo who formed the link between us: her husband and my brother, the man loved by each of us in our own way. As for Théo, he became an adult during his military service. On his return from

Algeria, he concentrated all his vital energy on the little time he had left to live, those years during which he gave Edith all the love he had received at the same time as he rose to the highest step on the artistic podium.

Many books have been published about Edith, most of them painting a rather depressing portrait of her; in general, they emphasise her deprived childhood, her ill health, her mood swings, the tragedies which punctuated her journey through life. For my part, I can say that I knew Edith at the height of her glory. The Piaf whose life I shared was an accomplished woman who had reached the height of her career, a superstar playing her role to perfection and rejoicing in the freedom she had earned. Yes, she was sick. Her liver was destroyed. She was exhausted. Age had begun to cause its damage. But it was her privilege to remain young at heart, which is why she was open to one last love affair.

For that's what I witnessed when I shared the lives of Edith and Théo: true love. Even if all of their words and deeds were observed by the press, the true nature of their relationship was very far from what the journalists were shown. They didn't live for appearances. They weren't trying to get their union caught in the limelight whenever they could. On the contrary, they yearned for calm and intimacy. They knew that they were not together by chance, but from the effect of a higher will than their own. And both of them knew instinctively that their time was limited. That's why, as with lovers the world over, they only wanted to be together, to make the most of each other, to live each moment to the full without worrying about the next day.

Both of them knew that love is what counts the most, and that love comes from God.

Cet ouvrage a été composé et mis en pages
par Facompo
à Lisieux (Calvados)
pour le compte des Éditions de l'Archipel
département éditorial
de la S.A.S. Écriture-Communication

CPSIA information can be obtained
at www.ICGtesting.com
Printed in the USA
LVHW02s0445261217
560802LV00019B/546/P

9 782809 815924